ham lyn
Qui ckCook

hamlyn

QuickCook
Low Fat

Recipes by Jo McAuley

Every dish, three ways—you choose!
30 minutes | 20 minutes | 10 minutes

An Hachette UK company
www.hachette.co.uk

First published in Great Britain in 2012 by Hamlyn,
a division of Octopus Publishing Group Ltd
Endeavour House, 189 Shaftesbury Avenue, London WC2H 8JY UK
www.octopusbooks.co.uk

Distributed in the US by Hachette Book Group USA
237 Park Avenue, New York, NY 10017 USA
www.octopusbooksusa.com

Distributed in Canada by Canadian Manda Group
165 Dufferin Street, Toronto, Ontario, Canada M6K 3H6

ISBN: 978-0-60062-401-1

Printed and bound in China

1 2 3 4 5 6 7 8 9 10

Ovens should be preheated to the specified temperature. If using a convection oven,
follow the manufacturer's instructions for adjusting the time and temperature.

This book contains some dishes made with raw or lightly cooked eggs. It is prudent
for more vulnerable people, such as pregnant and breastfeeding mothers, invalids,
the elderly, babies, and young children, to avoid uncooked or lightly cooked dishes
made with eggs.

This book includes dishes made with nuts and nut derivatives. It is advisable for those
with known allergic reactions to nuts and nut derivatives and those who may be
potentially vulnerable to these allergies, such as pregnant and breastfeeding
mothers, invalids, the elderly, babies, and children, to avoid dishes made with nuts
and nut oils. It is also prudent to check the labels of prepared ingredients for the
possible inclusion of nut derivatives.

Contents

Introduction

30 20 10—quick, quicker, quickest

This book offers a new and flexible approach to meal planning for busy cooks and lets you choose the recipe option that fits the time you have available the best. Inside you will find 360 dishes that will inspire you and motivate you to get cooking every day of the year. All the recipes take a maximum of 30 minutes to cook. Some take as few as 20 minutes and, amazingly, many take only 10 minutes. With a little preparation, you can easily try out one new recipe from this book each night and slowly you will build a wide and exciting portfolio of recipes to suit your needs.

How does it work?

Every recipe in the QuickCook series can be cooked one of three ways—a 30-minute version, a 20-minute version, or a super-quick and easy 10-minute version. At the beginning of each chapter you'll find recipes listed by time. Choose a dish based on how much time you have and turn to that page.

You'll find the main recipe in the middle of the page with a beautiful photograph and two time variations below.

If you enjoy the dish, you can go back and cook it using the other time options. If you liked the 30-minute Vanilla, Bran, and Blueberry Muffins, but only have 10 minutes to spare, then you'll find a way to cook it using cheat ingredients or handy shortcuts.

If you love the ingredients and flavors of the 10-minute Pan-Fried Salmon with Mixed Bean Salad, go ahead and try something more substantial like the 20-minute Baked Salmon and Mixed Beans, or be inspired to cook a more elaborate version like a Bean and Couscous Salad with Flaked Salmon. Alternatively, browse through all of the 360 delicious recipes. Find something that catches your eye, then cook the version that fits your time frame.

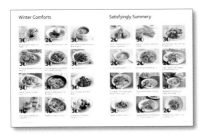

Or, for easy inspiration, turn to the gallery on pages 12–19 to get an instant overview by themes, such as Winter Comforts or Special Ocassions.

QuickCook online

And to make life even easier, you can use the special code on each recipe page to email yourself a recipe card for printing, or email a text-only grocery list to your cell. Go to www.hamlynquickcook.com and enter the recipe code at the bottom of each page.

LOW-LIG-QEW

QuickCook Low Fat

Trying to stick to a diet low in fat can be difficult. People often think that if they leave out all the "bad stuff" then mealtimes will become boring and not substantial enough to keep them satisfied throughout the day. This leaves them with low energy levels and an increased likelihood to snack. The willpower so necessary in any kind of weight loss program can quickly fade and the pounds we have worked so hard to lose are quickly regained as we return to our old eating habits.

It has been proven that losing weight slowly and sensibly, through a combination of healthy eating and exercise, is not only much better for our general health but also that, once we have lost the weight, we are much more likely to keep it off. So, in order to help you succeed in hitting your own weight-loss target and live a healthier life, this book is crammed with low-fat, nutritious, and substantial recipes. They are not only healthy and delicious but also designed to suit any budget, time frame, or level of expertise. Whether you are cooking for guests with different dietary needs or just looking for enjoyable family suppers, you will find these recipes flexible enough to suit any occasion. Sticking to a diet low in fat will be easier than you imagined.

Tips and Techniques

Changing the way you cook can dramatically reduce the amount of added fat you use. So rather than frying food in a lot of oil, try adopting a different cooking method:

- Stir-frying in a hot wok requires a lot less oil and also retains more nutrients than many other ways of cooking.
- Steaming food in a basket or electric steamer uses no oil or added fat at all and is an extremely healthy way to cook.
- Gently poaching is a great, low-fat way of cooking meat and fish while keeping it tender and moist.
- Cooking food under a broiler or on a ridged griddle pan also uses less fat than frying. It allows excess fat to melt away, gives food a lovely grilled taste, and will "crisp" certain foods such as meat, in a way that some other low-fat cooking methods can't.
- Try using a light oil spray to grease your pans rather than butter or oil. It enables you to fry or roast food without adding too much fat.
- Using a microwave to defrost and reheat food saves time and effort. Try cooking vegetables in a microwave to retain nutrients.
- Cooking food in a pressure cooker will dramatically reduce cooking times and can make your life much easier.
- Try using a flat or ridged panini machine to cook food. Both sides cook at once, so this will cut the cooking time in half.

There a few simple cooking aids that really can have an amazing effect on the time spent in the kitchen.

- A food processor and a mini chopper are both really useful pieces of equipment and are great time-savers.

- Handheld mixers and jug blenders will puree sauces and soups almost instantly.

- A good vegetable peeler, a garlic peeler, and a crusher are all great, simple little gadgets to help save time on fiddly jobs.

- Using a mandolin slicer to slice vegetables is flexible and fast and will save a lot of time when preparing food.

- Good, sharp knives make food preparation simpler and faster. If your knives are too blunt, use a knife sharpener to sharpen them.

- Try cooking large amounts and then freezing in portions. This way, you'll always have a fast, ready-made, low-effort meal at your fingertips.

- Preparing ingredients in advance will save time when you come to cook the meal later on. Peel and chop vegetables ahead of time, for example, then keep them refrigerated in sealed freezer bags until you need them.

Ingredients and Kitchen Cupboard

To reduce the amount of time spent preparing and cooking, see what healthy alternatives there are available to replace certain ingredients. It is worth remembering that anything prepared ahead of time this way will usually be more expensive. However, waste is minimal, so you will often find it all balances out.

- Try using precooked meats and fish, such as roast chicken or canned tuna.

- Use frozen prepared vegetables, such as chopped spinach. Frozen vegetables are easy to use and are high in nutrients.

- Buy meat that has been been trimmed of excess fat and cut into strips or cubes. This way it is ready to add to a recipe, saving on time and waste.

- Buying a bag of pre-prepared stir-fry vegetables or trimmed, washed, and ready-to-cook vegetables will reduce the amount of preparation necessary. The same applies to prepared bags of washed salad greens.

- Jars of minced herbs, ginger, garlic, chiles, and lemon grass can all be used as substitutes for the "real thing" and will save on time.

- You can try using ready-made sauces and dressings but take the time to read the ingredients list and nutritional information to make sure there are not too many fats and hidden calories.

- Presteamed rice, couscous, pastas, and grains, as well as canned legumes, make a great foundation for an almost instant meal.

Winter Comforts

Comforting food for a cold winter's day.

Vanilla, Bran, and Blueberry
Muffins 28

Crunchy Cinnamon French
Toast 36

Semidried Tomato and Italian
Bean Soup 60

Hot Smoked Trout and Potato
Salad 68

Pork and Rosemary Meatballs
with Mixed Bean Salad 150

Chili Con Carne 154

Mild and Creamy Chicken
Curry 168

Madeira and Rosemary Pork
Medallions 194

Meaty Mushrooms in Red
Wine 230

Quick Spiced Rhubarb and
Ginger Fool 268

Raspberry Yogurt Gratin 274

Mulled Wine Dried Fruit
Compote 278

Satisfyingly Summery

Fresh flavors that capture summer on a plate.

Chunky Fruit Skewers with Rosewater Dressing 30

Butternut Squash and Ricotta Frittata 52

Warm Rainbow Salad with New Potatoes 56

Great Chilled Gazpacho 66

Tomato and Bread Soup 72

Cajun-Spiced Jumbo Shrimp with Mixed Rice 100

Red Mullet with Capers and a Warm Tomato Salad 104

Sweet Chile Chicken Stir-Fry 156

Stuffed Pork Steaks with Lima Bean Salad 188

Grilled Vegetable Salad 236

Creamy Stuffed Roast Peppers with Mixed Grains 240

Mediterranean Bowl of Giant Couscous 244

Good For Lunch

Healthy dishes for a tasty lunchtime treat.

Whole-Wheat Bagel with Scrambled Eggs and Smoked Salmon 24

Grilled Sourdough with Herby Ricotta and Pancetta 46

Grilled Mushroom and Garlic Wraps 50

Roasted Peppers on Rye 80

Hot and Sour Shrimp Soup 90

Soy and Ginger Tuna Fishcakes 98

Smoked Mackerel Pasta Salad 124

Chinese Chicken Wraps with Plum Sauce 148

Serrano Ham and Watercress Salad with Avocado 186

Quinoa-Stuffed Tomatoes with Melting Mozzarella 204

Green Lentil Tapenade with Toast 214

More Than 5 Vegetable Pizza 220

Treats for the Weekend

Inspiring meals for something a bit different.

Potato and Sweetcorn Hash with Frazzled Eggs 32

Pancakes with Bacon and Maple Syrup 48

Baked Haddock with Garlic Crumb Crust 126

Tandoori Chicken Skewers with Cucumber Salad 140

Turkey Burger with Spicy Salsa 152

"Meat Feast" Thin and Crispy Pizza 158

Lebanese Lamb Skewers with Cucumber Salad 170

Fast-Seared Steak with French Beans 176

Grilled Barbecue Pork with Coleslaw 198

Lemon Yogurt Cupcakes 258

Blueberry and Orange Eton Mess 260

Individual Chocolate Pots 262

Special Occasions

Spectacular dishes for entertaining without the high-fat content.

Mixed Rice and Bean Salad with Smoked Duck Breast 78

Aromatic Steamed Mussels 106

Grilled Scallops with Chermoula Dressing 116

"Roast" Spiced Tuna Loin with Potatoes and Asparagus 128

Griddled Salmon Fillet with Potatoes and Beans 132

Baked Chicken Parcels with Mozzarella and Pesto 160

Roast Pork Tenderloin with Lemon, Sage, and Capers 184

Poached Poussin with Baby Vegetables 192

Turkey Breast with Prosciutto 196

Individual Baked Strawberry and Lemon Meringues 250

Baked Figs with Sauternes 266

Baked Nectarines with Vanilla and Cointreau 276

Low Carb

Low-fat and low-carb recipes that don't compromise on flavor.

20

Smoked Ham and Cherry Tomato Omelet 44

20

Butterflied Sardines with Beet Salsa 56

30

Smoked Chicken with Beans, Walnuts, and Tarragon 74

10

Real Guacamole with Raw Vegetables 76

10

Pan-Fried Salmon with Mixed Bean Salad 88

20

Baked Sea Bream with Cumin and Cucumber Yogurt 96

10

Swordfish Steaks with Basil and Pine Nut Oil 102

10

Lemony Scallop Skewers with Arugula 130

30

Asian-Spiced Beef Carpaccio 142

30

Rare Beef and Baby Beet Salad 146

20

Honey and Mustard Chicken Fillets with Coleslaw 164

10

Marinated Tofu with Sesame Seeds 222

Fabulously Fruity

Fresh flavors with a fruity twist.

Apple and Yogurt Granola 26

Pomegranate and Granola Smoothie 34

Prune and Banana Crunch 40

Lime and Ginger Coleslaw with 5-Spiced Shrimp 70

Grilled Sardines with Mango and Lime Salsa 92

Moroccan Grilled Lamb with Golden Raisins 180

Watermelon, Pomegranate, and Halloumi Salad 210

Fragrant Poached Apricots with Pistachios 252

Fresh Berries with Crunchy Oats 254

Sweet and Sour Spiced Pineapple and Mango 256

Cinnamon and Raisin Pear Trifle 264

Quick Kiwifruit and Ginger Cheesecake 272

Pasta, Noodles, and Rice

Fabulous recipe ideas using kitchen-cupboard staples.

Fragrant Soba Noodle Soup 82

Skewered Teriyaki Cod with Steamed Ginger Rice 110

Pasta with Tuna and Aubergine Arrabiata 134

5-Spiced Duck with Ramen Noodles 166

Gnocchi with Smoked Turkey and Blue Cheese 174

Quick Beef Bolognaise 182

Chicken Risotto with White Wine and Asparagus 190

Chile-Spiked Broccoli with Linguine 206

One-Pot Southern-Style Rice 212

Penne in Tomato, Artichoke, and Olive Sauce 216

Vietnamese-Style Vegetable Noodle Salad 228

Lemony Pea and Ricotta Risotto 238

QuickCook

Breakfast and Light Bites

Recipes listed by cooking time

30

20

Whole-Wheat Bagel with Scrambled Eggs and Hot-Smoked Salmon

Serves 4

4 hot-smoked salmon fillets, about 4½ oz each

8 eggs

½ cup lowfat milk

1 tablespoon chopped chervil

1 tablespoon snipped chives, plus 2 tablespoons extra to garnish

1 tablespoon low-fat spread

4 whole-wheat or multigrain bagels, cut in a half

5 tablespoons extra-light cream cheese or ricotta

salt and pepper

- Arrange the smoked salmon fillets on a foil-lined cookie sheet, cover with more foil, and place in a preheated oven at 350°F for 12–15 minutes or until heated through.

- Meanwhile, beat together in a bowl the eggs, milk, and herbs. Season with salt and pepper.

- Melt the low-fat spread in a large, nonstick saucepan over medium-low heat until frothy, then pour in the egg mixture. Turn the temperature down to very low and, using a heat-resistant spatula, stir the eggs gently for 5–6 minutes, or until they are creamy.

- Spilt and toast the bagels, spread the bases thinly with the cream cheese, and then spoon over the scrambled eggs.

- Flake the hot-smoked salmon fillets over the scrambled eggs, garnish them with the snipped chives and black pepper, and serve.

 Smoked Salmon with Herbed Scrambled Eggs Beat 8 eggs, ½ cup lowfat milk, 1 tablespoon chopped chervil, and 1 tablespoon chopped chives together in a bowl, then cook as above. Meanwhile, toast 4 halved bagels under a medium broiler or in a toaster. Spoon the scrambled eggs over the toasted bagel halves and top with 4 slices of thinly sliced smoked salmon. Garnish with snipped chives and serve immediately.

 Poached Eggs with Roasted Smoked Salmon Place 4 lightly smoked salmon fillets in a small, foil-lined roasting pan. Sprinkle over 1 tablespoon chopped chervil, 1 tablespoon snipped chives, and some black pepper. Then drizzle with 1 tablespoon canola oil. Roast in a preheated oven at 400°F for 15–18 minutes until just cooked. Meanwhile, poach 4 eggs, 2 at a time, in a large pan of simmering water for 3 minutes. Arrange 2 large handfuls of mixed watercress, arugula, and baby spinach over 4 serving plates. Flake over the roasted salmon and top each plate with a poached egg. Garnish with snipped chives and black pepper and serve with halved toasted bagels.

10 Apple and Yogurt Granola

Serves 4

3 cups fruit and nut granola (preferably no added sugar)

2 all-purpose apples, such as Granny Smiths, peeled and coarsely grated

2 cups chilled apple juice

1 cup fat-free Greek-style yogurt with honey

2 teaspoons golden flax seeds (optional)

honey (optional)

- Place the granola in a bowl and mix with the grated apples. Pour over the apple juice, stir well to combine, and leave to soak for 5–6 minutes.

- Divide the soaked granola into serving bowls and spoon the yogurt on top of each one. Scatter over the flax seeds, if using, and serve drizzled with some honey, if liked.

20 Apple Bircher Muesli

Soak 3 cups fruit and nut granola in 2 cups hot lowfat milk for 15 minutes while the milk cools. Divide into serving bowls and spoon over 1 cup low-fat yogurt. Top each bowl with grated apple from 2 all-purpose apples and serve sprinkled with 2 teaspoons golden flax seeds and a drizzle of honey, if liked.

30 Granola Scones with Apple and Yogurt

Mix 1½ generous cups self-rising flour with a pinch of salt in a large bowl. Rub in 3½ tablespoons chilled butter and add 2 tablespoons golden granulated sugar. Stir in ½ cup lowfat milk to form a soft dough, adding 1 tablespoon more milk if necessary. Knead lightly, then place on a lightly floured surface and pat to a thickness of ¾ inch. Use a 2 inch cookie cutter to cut the dough into 8–10 rounds, gathering up any remaining dough to make more scones. Place on a lightly greased cookie sheet, brush with a little extra milk, sprinkle over 2 tablespoons fruit and nut granola, and bake in a preheated oven at 425°F for about 12 minutes, or until risen and golden. Remove and transfer to a wire rack to cool slightly, then split the scones in half. Serve with grated apple, Greek-style yogurt with honey, and golden flax seeds, as liked.

Vanilla, Bran, and Blueberry Muffins

Makes 12 muffins

2 cups all-purpose flour
1 cup bran
1 teaspoon baking powder
1 teaspoon baking soda
3 eggs
1 teaspoon vanilla extract
1 cup lowfat buttermilk
¼ cup rice bran oil or peanut oil
1 cup blueberries

- Preheat the oven to 350°F and lightly grease a 12-cup, nonstick muffin pan or line the muffin pan with paper bake cases.

- In a large bowl mix together the dry ingredients until well combined. Break the eggs into a large jug and beat lightly, then add the vanilla extract, buttermilk, and oil.

- Pour the egg mixture into the dry ingredients, add the blueberries, and fold gently using a large, metal spoon just until barely combined.

- Spoon the batter evenly between the muffin cups.

- Bake in the oven for 18–20 minutes, until risen, golden, and firm. Remove from the oven and transfer to a wire rack to cool slightly before serving warm.

 Healthy Blueberry Smoothie

Place 1¾ cups blueberries in a blender with 1 cup bran, ½ cup lowfat buttermilk, 2 scoops low-fat ice cream, 1 teaspoon vanilla extract, and 2½ cups lowfat milk. Blend until smooth and serve.

 Toasted Blueberry and Seed Granola

Pour 1 cup bran into a large skillet over medium heat and dry-fry, stirring frequently, until toasted. Tip into a bowl and then repeat the toasting process with 1½ cups rolled oats, followed by ⅓ cup sunflower seeds, scant ½ cup pumpkin seeds, and ¾ cup roughly chopped pecan nuts. Add a generous ½ cup dried blueberries and 2 tablespoons dried goji berries or sour cherries to the bowl with the toasted ingredients. Stir until well combined. When completely cool, store the granola in an airtight container. To serve, stir 1 teaspoon vanilla extract into the desired quantity of lowfat milk and pour over bowls of granola.

LOW-LIGH-XIL

Chunky Fruit Skewers with Rosewater Dressing

Serves 4

1½ cups guava, apple, or
  raspberry and guava juice

2 tablespoons rosewater

3 cardamom pods, lightly crushed

2 star anise

2 tablespoons soft light
  brown sugar

1 papaya, cut in half, seeded, and
  cut into chunks

2 kiwifruit, peeled and cut
  into chunks

1 small pineapple, peeled, cored,
  and cut into chunks

1¾ cups strawberries, hulled, and
  cut in half if large

- Pour the fruit juice and rosewater into a small saucepan, add the cardamom, star anise, and sugar, and place over low heat. Stir to dissolve the sugar, then simmer gently for 5–6 minutes until fragrant. Pour into a large, shallow bowl and set aside to cool.

- Meanwhile, thread the chunks of papaya, kiwifruit, and pineapple alternately onto 8 skewers. Arrange 2 skewers per person on serving plates.

- Strain the dressing into a jug to remove the spices and drizzle over the fruit skewers before serving.

Tropical Fruit and Rosewater Juice

Prepare ½ small pineapple, 2 kiwifruit, 1 papaya, and 1¾ cups strawberries, as above, and put in a blender with a pinch of ground cardamom and 3 cups guava juice. Blend until smooth, then stir in 2 tablespoons rosewater. Fill tall glasses with ice cubes, add 1 whole star anise to each glass, and then pour in the fruit juice. Serve immediately.

Mixed Fruit Crisp with Spicy Guava Syrup

Mix together in a large bowl ¾ cups all-purpose flour and ½ teaspoon ground ginger. Stir in 3½ tablespoons melted butter, ¾ cup rolled oats, ¼ cup Demerara sugar, and 2 tablespoons desiccated coconut. In another bowl, toss together 1 pineapple, 2 kiwifruit, 1 papaya, and 1¾ cups strawberries, prepared as above. Tip the fruits into an ovenproof dish, scatter the oat topping evenly over the top, and gently press down. Bake in a preheated oven at 400°F for about 20 minutes or until the fruit is tender and the topping crunchy. Meanwhile, make the spiced syrup as above, using 1½ cups guava juice, 2 tablespoons rosewater, 3 lightly crushed cardamom pods, 2 star anise, and 2 tablespoons soft light brown sugar. Serve the crisp drizzled with the warm syrup and a dollop of fat-free Greek-style yogurt. Sprinkle over desiccated coconut and drizzle with liquid honey, if liked.

LOW-LIGH-XYL

Potato and Sweetcorn Hash with Frazzled Eggs

Serves 4

1½ lb large potatoes, peeled and diced

2 tablespoons light olive oil

1 large onion, finely chopped

1 large green pepper, seeded and chopped

1 teaspoon smoked paprika

7 oz can corn, drained

olive oil spray

4 large eggs

2 tablespoons snipped chives

salt and pepper

- Put the potatoes in a large saucepan and cover with lightly salted water. Bring to a boil and cook for 12–15 minutes until tender, then drain in a colander.

- Meanwhile, heat the oil in a large, nonstick ovenproof skillet over medium heat. Add the onion and green pepper and cook, stirring occasionally, for 7–8 minutes until softened and lightly golden. Add the cooked potatoes, smoked paprika, and corn, season generously with salt and pepper, and cook for 3–4 minutes, stirring frequently.

- Slide the pan under a preheated broiler and broil for 2–3 minutes until crisp.

- While the hash is broiling, spray a large skillet with the oil then place over a medium heat. Crack the eggs into the pan and fry for 3 minutes until the egg whites are set and crisp.

- Using a lifter, lift the eggs onto the hash in the pan and place under the broiler once again to cook the yolk, if desired. Serve immediately sprinkled with the snipped chives.

 Warm Salad with Frazzled Eggs

Fry 1 finely chopped onion and 1 chopped green pepper in 1 tablespoon oil, as above. One minute before the end of cooking, add a 7 oz can corn, drained, and 1 teaspoon smoked paprika. Meanwhile "frazzle" the eggs as above. Toss the vegetables with 2 handfuls crunchy lettuce greens and 1 tablespoon red wine vinegar. Arrange on serving plates and top the salad with a frazzled egg. Serve sprinkled with snipped chives.

 Spanish-Style Sweetcorn Tortilla

Thinly slice 1 lb small potatoes and cook in lightly salted boiling water for 10–12 minutes until tender. Meanwhile, fry 1 finely chopped large onion and 1 large seeded and chopped green pepper in 1 tablespoon light olive oil, as above. Add 1 teaspoon smoked paprika and a 7 oz can of corn, drained, and cook for a further minute. Beat 6 eggs in a bowl and season generously with salt and pepper. Drain the potatoes and stir into the pan with the onions and peppers. Add the eggs, cover loosely, and cook for 3–4 minutes, without stirring. Invert the tortilla onto a plate and slide it back into the pan for a further 3–4 minutes until firm. Slide onto a large plate and serve in wedges.

10 Pomegranate and Granola Smoothie

Serves 4

3 cups pomegranate juice

2 tablespoons pomegranate molasses

1 lb fresh or frozen mango pieces

1 cup granola

1–2 tablespoons agave nectar or liquid honey

4 scoops fat-free frozen yogurt

½ heaped cup pomegranate seeds (optional)

- Place all the ingredients except the frozen yogurt and pomegranate seeds, if using, in a blender and blend until smooth. This may need to be done in 2 batches.

- Take 4 glasses and place 1 scoop of frozen yogurt in each. Pour the smoothie over the yogurt, sprinkle over pomegranate seeds, if using, and serve immediately.

 Fruit Salad with Pomegranate Syrup

Place 1½ cups pomegranate juice in a saucepan with 1–2 tablespoons agave nectar or liquid honey, to taste, and the seeds scraped from 1 vanilla pod. Simmer for 4–5 minutes until thickened, then remove from the heat. Meanwhile, peel and cut up the flesh of ¼ watermelon into large chunks, removing any seeds. Mix with 2 cups halved seedless grapes, 2 cups fresh or frozen mango pieces, and 2 peeled and thickly sliced kiwifruit in a large bowl. Spoon into serving dishes and top with a scoop of fat-free frozen yogurt, if liked. Scatter with heaping ½ cup pomegranate seeds, if liked, and drizzle with 2 tablespoons pomegranate syrup. Serve immediately.

 Quinoa Porridge with Pomegranate

Place 1½ cups uncooked quinoa in a saucepan with 4 cups lowfat milk, 1–2 tablespoons agave nectar or liquid honey, to taste, and 2 tablespoons pomegranate molasses. Bring to a boil, cover, reduce the heat to low, and simmer gently, stirring occasionally, for 15–20 minutes until tender and creamy. Stir in 1 teaspoon rosewater and then spoon into serving bowls. Serve with a spoonful of fat-free Greek-style yogurt and scattered with heaping ½ cup pomegranate seeds.

Crunchy Cinnamon French Toast

Serves 4

3 eggs
¼ lowfat milk
½ teaspoon ground cinnamon
2 tablespoons butter
8 slices raisin and cinnamon bread
  or 4 low-fat hot cross buns
8 tablespoons Demerara or
  cinnamon sugar
4 scoops of low-fat ice-cream
  or frozen yogurt, to serve
  (optional)

- In a large, shallow bowl, beat the eggs with the milk and cinnamon. Melt half the butter in a large, nonstick skillet over medium heat.

- Dip 4 slices of the bread in the egg mixture and sprinkle both sides with half the sugar. Alternatively, cut the hot cross buns in half horizontally and dip 4 halves in the egg and then sprinkle with the sugar.

- Place the coated bread in the melted butter and cook gently for 4–6 minutes, turning once, until golden and crisp. Drain on paper towels and keep warm. Repeat the process with the remaining slices of bread.

- Serve 2 slices of French toast per person with a scoop of ice-cream or frozen yogurt.

 Crunchy Granola with Cinnamon and Apple Divide 2¾ cups crunchy granola among 4 bowls. Peel, core, and dice 2 all-purpose apples, such as Granny Smiths, and scatter the apple over the granola with ½ cup golden raisins. Stir 1 teaspoon ground cinnamon into 1 cup fat-free Greek-style yogurt with honey, then spoon into the bowls. Serve sprinkled with cinnamon sugar, if liked.

 Cinnamon and Raisin Pastries Beat 1 egg with 1 tablespoon lowfat milk and brush over a 12 oz rectangle of ready-rolled, low-fat puff pastry. Scatter over 1 teaspoon ground cinnamon, ½ cup golden raisins, and 4 tablespoons cinnamon sugar. Roll up the pastry and cut into ½ inch rounds. Place the rounds on a large, lightly greased cookie sheet, leaving space for them to expand. Flatten the rounds slightly and brush them again with the remaining egg wash. Sprinkle with 1 tablespoon cinnamon sugar and cook in a preheated oven at 400°C for about 20 minutes, or until crisp and golden.

3 Moroccan Baked Eggs

Serves 4

1 tablespoon olive oil
1 onion, chopped
2 garlic cloves, sliced
1 teaspoon ras el hanout
¼ teaspoon ground cinnamon
1 teaspoon ground coriander
1 lb 12 oz can cherry tomatoes
4 tablespoons chopped cilantro
4 eggs
salt and pepper

- Preheat the oven to 425°F. Heat the olive oil in a skillet over medium heat, add the onion and garlic, and cook for 6–7 minutes, or until softened and lightly golden, stirring occasionally.

- Stir in the spices and cook for a further minute, then add the cherry tomatoes. Season generously with salt and pepper, then simmer gently for 8–10 minutes. Scatter over 3 tablespoons of the cilantro.

- Divide the tomato mixture into 4 individual ovenproof dishes, then crack an egg into each dish. Cook in the oven for 8–10 minutes until the egg is set but the yolks are still slightly runny. Cook for a further 2–3 minutes if you prefer the eggs to be cooked through.

- Serve scattered with the remaining cilantro and plenty of crusty bread on the side.

1 Moroccan Fried Eggs with Spinach

Heat 1 tablespoon olive oil in a large skillet over medium heat. Add 1 teaspoon ras el hanout, ¼ teaspoon ground cinnamon, and 1 teaspoon ground coriander. Fry for 1 minute. Crack 4 eggs into the pan and cook for 3–5 minutes, or until cooked to your liking. Meanwhile, toast 4 slices of crusty bread and place a handful of baby spinach on each. Scatter over 4 halved cherry tomatoes per person and sprinkle over chopped cilantro. Lift the fried eggs onto the spinach and serve.

2 Pan-Baked Moroccan Eggs

Heat 1 tablespoon olive oil in a skillet over medium heat. Add 1 chopped onion and 2 sliced garlic cloves and cook for 6–7 minutes until softened. Add 1 teaspoon ras el hanout, ¼ teaspoon ground cinnamon, and 1 teaspoon ground coriander. Cook for 1 minute, then add a 1 lb 12 oz can cherry tomatoes and season with salt and pepper. Gently simmer for about 6–7 minutes or until fragrant, then add 3 tablespoons chopped cilantro. Make 4 shallow wells in the surface of the tomato sauce and crack an egg into each. Cover the pan with a lid and cook for 3–4 minutes or until the eggs are cooked to your liking. Transfer to serving plates with 1 egg per person, scatter over 1 tablespoon chopped cilantro, and serve.

10 Prune and Banana Crunch

Serves 4

2 firm, ripe bananas, diced

2 cups ready-to-eat pitted prunes

2 teaspoons liquid honey (optional)

2 cups fat-free Greek-style yogurt

2 cups cornflakes or crunchy cereal flakes

- Combine the bananas, prunes, honey, and yogurt in a large bowl.

- Spoon into attractive glass bowls and top with the cornflakes or crunchy cereal flakes. Serve immediately with glasses of apple juice, if liked.

2 Banana Yogurt and Prune Compote

with Granola Roughly chop 2 cups ready-to-eat pitted prunes and place in a small pan with ¾ cup prune juice, 2 teaspoons liquid honey, finely grated zest of ½ orange, 2 cloves, and ½ cinnamon stick. Place over low heat and simmer for 5–6 minutes until thick and sticky. Set aside to cool for 8–10 minutes. While cooling, mash 2 firm, ripe bananas into 2 cups fat-free Greek-style yogurt. Spoon the banana yogurt into serving bowls over the desired amounts of healthy granola. Remove the whole spices from the prune compote and spoon over the yogurt. Serve immediately.

3 Banana and Prune Muffins

Put 2 cups self-rising flour, 1 teaspoon baking powder, ⅔ cup soft dark brown sugar, 2 lightly beaten eggs, ¾ cup lowfat milk, ¼ vegetable oil, 1 mashed banana, and ⅔ cup chopped, ready-to-eat stoned prunes into a large bowl. Beat to combine, then spoon into the cups of a lightly greased nonstick 12-cup muffin pan. Cook in a preheated oven at 400°F for 18–20 minutes until golden, risen, and firm to the touch. Remove from the oven and transfer to a wire rack to cool slightly before serving.

Giant Apple and Cinnamon Muffins

Makes 6

butter, for greasing
1 ⅔ cups whole-wheat flour
¾ cup fine oatmeal
1 teaspoon baking powder
1 teaspoon baking soda
½ teaspoon ground cinnamon
½ cup soft light brown sugar
pinch of salt
7 oz apple, apple and apricot, or
   apple and blueberry purée
⅔ cup buttermilk
3 tablespoons peanut oil
2 large eggs, lightly beaten

- Preheat the oven to 350°F and lightly grease a 6-hole nonstick giant muffin pan.

- In a large bowl, mix together all the dry ingredients.

- Beat the remaining ingredients together in a jug and pour into the dry mixture. Use a large metal spoon to stir until barely combined, then divide the batter into the holes of the prepared muffin pan. Place in the oven for 20–22 minutes until risen, firm, and golden. Remove from the oven and let sit briefly in the muffin pan before transferring the muffins to a wire rack to cool slightly. Serve while still warm.

 Apple and Cinnamon Oaty Yogurt

Mix together 7 oz apple purée and ½ teaspoon cinnamon in a bowl, then fold into 1¼ cups fat-free Greek-style yogurt with honey. Serve sprinkled with ½ cup rolled oats and a little soft light brown sugar, if liked.

 Cinnamon Stewed Apples

Peel, core, and dice 3 all-purpose apples, about 1 lb total weight. Place in a saucepan with ½ teaspoon cinnamon, 2 tablespoons soft light brown sugar, and 1 tablespoon apple juice. Warm over medium heat for 5–6 minutes until the apples collapse. Cool slightly, then serve with the desired quantity of healthy granola.

# 2 Smoked Ham and Cherry Tomato Omelet

Serves 4

4 teaspoons canola oil
4 shallots, thinly sliced
8 eggs, lightly beaten
2 tablespoons chopped mixed
  herbs, such as chives, chervil,
  parsley, basil, and thyme
1¼ cups yellow and red cherry
  tomatoes, cut in half
5 oz wafer-thin slices
  smoked ham
salt and pepper

- Heat 1 teaspoon of the oil in a medium-sized skillet over medium-low heat. Add the shallots and cook gently for 4–5 minutes or until softened.

- Meanwhile, beat together the eggs and herbs in a large jug and season with salt and pepper.

- Remove three-quarters of the shallots from the pan with a slotted spoon and pour over one-quarter of the egg mixture. Scatter over one-quarter of the cherry tomatoes and stir gently, using a heat-resistant rubber spatula, until the egg is almost set.

- Scatter one-quarter of the sliced ham evenly over the top of the omelet and cook gently for a further minute. Fold the omelet in half and slide out of the pan onto a warmed plate. Serve immediately and repeat the process to make 3 more omelets. Alternatively, keep the cooked omelets warm until all 4 are ready and serve at the same time.

Smoked Ham and Tomato Frittata

In a large ovenproof skillet melt 1 tablespoon butter over medium heat until frothy. Add 8 lightly beaten eggs to the pan, 2 tablespoons chopped mixed herbs, selection as above, and 1¼ cups halved yellow and red cherry tomatoes. Gently stir together. Add 5 oz roughly chopped wafer-thin slices smoked ham and continue stirring gently for 2–3 minutes until almost set. Sprinkle over 2 tablespoons grated Parmesan cheese, then place under a preheated medium broiler for 3–4 minutes until set and golden. Serve in wedges with salad greens.

Smoked Ham and Tomato Flan

Beat 6 eggs with 2 tablespoons chopped mixed herbs, selection as above, and season with salt and pepper. Spread 5 oz wafer-thin slices smoked ham over the base of a 9 inch prebaked pastry case, then pour in the egg mixture. Scatter over 1¼ cups halved cherry tomatoes, then sprinkle over 2 tablespoons grated Parmesan cheese. Place in a preheated oven at 400°F for 20–25 minutes until set and golden.

 # Grilled Sourdough with Herby Ricotta and Crisp Pancetta

Serves 4

4 large slices sourdough bread

8 slices lean pancetta

1 cup ready-to-eat, slow-roasted tomatoes (not in oil), chopped

2 tablespoons toasted pine nuts (optional)

arugula, to garnish

Herby Ricotta Filling

1 cup ricotta or extra-light cream cheese

2 scallions, finely chopped

4 tablespoons chopped mixed herbs, such as chervil, chives, parsley, basil, marjoram, and tarragon

finely grated zest of 1 lemon

1 tablespoon lemon juice

salt and pepper

- For the herby ricotta filling, mix together the ricotta or cream cheese with the scallions, mixed herbs, and lemon zest and juice. Season with salt and pepper and set aside.

- Heat a ridged griddle pan and toast the slices of bread in 2 batches for 3–4 minutes each batch, turning once, or until toasted and lightly charred. Keep warm.

- Leave the pan on the heat and add the pancetta. Griddle for 2–3 minutes, turning once, until crisp. Drain any excess fat on paper towels.

- Spread the toast thickly with the ricotta mixture and arrange on serving plates. Scatter over the slow-roasted tomatoes and the pine nuts, if using, then top with the slices of crisp pancetta. Garnish with arugula and serve.

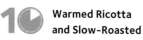 **Warmed Ricotta and Slow-Roasted Tomato Open Sandwiches**

Make up the herby ricotta filling, as above. Spread the ricotta over 4 large slices sourdough bread, then place on a broiler rack under a preheated medium broiler for 3 minutes until heated through. Remove and layer over 8 slices of lean Parma ham. Scatter with arugula and 1 cup chopped ready-to-eat, slow-roasted tomatoes (not in oil), and serve.

 Herby Ricotta Tomato Toasts

Make up the herby ricotta filling as above, then mix in 7 oz chopped, drained, roasted red peppers and 2 tablespoons toasted pine nuts. Cut the tops off 4 large beefsteak tomatoes and scoop out the seeds. Stuff the tomatoes with the ricotta filling and transfer the tomatoes to a baking pan. Bake in a preheated oven at 375°F for 20–22 minutes or until the tomatoes are tender. Meanwhile, griddle 4 large slices sourdough bread as above, then cut 1 garlic clove in half and rub the cut edges over the toasted bread. Grill 8 slices lean pancetta on the hot griddle pan until crisp. Serve the stuffed tomatoes on the garlicky toast, topped with crisp pancetta, and each one drizzled with 1 teaspoon balsamic syrup.

30 Pancakes with Bacon and Maple Syrup

Serves 4

1½ cups self-rising flour
1 teaspoon baking powder
pinch of cinnamon
1 egg, lightly beaten
⅔ cup buttermilk
½ cup lowfat milk
1 teaspoon vanilla extract
8 slices lean smoked bacon
1 tablespoon butter
2–4 tablespoons maple syrup,
    to serve

- Sift the flour, baking powder, and cinnamon into a bowl and make a well in the center. Pour in the eggs, buttermilk, lowfat milk, and vanilla extract. Beat to a smooth batter.

- Place the bacon on a foil-lined baking pan under a preheated broiler for 5–6 minutes or until the fat has melted away and the bacon is crisp. Keep warm.

- Melt a little butter in a large, nonstick skillet over medium heat and pour in 4 spoonfuls of the batter to make 4 small, thick pancakes. Cook for 2–3 minutes, then flip the pancakes over and cook for a further 2–3 minutes until golden. Remove and repeat the process to make 12 pancakes, or until the batter is finished, stacking up the pancakes, and keeping them warm in the oven.

- Serve the pancakes with the crisp bacon and drizzled with the maple syrup.

 Scotch Pancakes with Bacon and Maple Syrup Heat 8 ready-made Scotch pancakes according to the package instructions. Grill 8 bacon slices as in the 30-minute variation and serve with the warmed pancakes, drizzled with the maple syrup.

 Banana Pancakes and Maple Syrup Sift 1½ cups self-rising flour, 1 teaspoon baking powder, and a pinch of cinnamon into a bowl and mix with 1 tablespoon superfine sugar, 1 lightly beaten egg, ⅔ cup buttermilk, ½ cup lowfat milk, and 1 teaspoon vanilla extract to make a batter, as above. Mash 1 banana with a fork and stir into the batter with 1 scant cup raspberries. Cook the pancakes until golden, as above. Serve in stacks with low-fat ice-cream and drizzled with warmed maple syrup.

 # Grilled Mushroom and Garlic Wraps

Serves 4

1 lb large, flat field mushrooms, thickly sliced

2 garlic cloves, finely chopped

3 scallions, trimmed and thinly sliced

2 tablespoons olive oil

½ cup extra-light cream cheese

4 large, low-fat or multiseed soft tortilla wrap breads

4 tablespoons snipped chives

12 cherry tomatoes, cut into quarters

2 romaine lettuce hearts, shredded, plus extra to serve (optional)

salt and pepper

- Toss the mushrooms with the garlic, scallions, and olive oil in a large bowl. Season with salt and pepper, then tip onto a nonstick cookie sheet and place under a preheated medium broiler for 6–8 minutes until golden and tender, turning frequently.

- Meanwhile, spread the cream cheese over the tortilla wraps and scatter over the chives.

- Place the sliced mushrooms on the center of each wrap, then scatter over the cherry tomatoes, and top with a handful of the lettuce. Fold the edges of the wrap into the center to completely enclose the filling, creating 4 parcels.

- Heat a large, ridged griddle pan over medium-high heat. Place the parcels on the griddle and toast for 4–5 minutes, turning occasionally, until nicely charred on both sides. This may need to be done in 2 batches.

- Cut in half diagonally and serve immediately.

 **Quick Mushroom, Cream Cheese and Chive Wraps** Heat 1 tablespoon olive oil in a skillet over medium heat, and cook 1 lb thickly sliced, large, flat field mushrooms with 2 finely chopped garlic cloves for 5–6 minutes. Meanwhile, spread 4 low-fat soft tortilla wraps with ½ cup extra-light cream cheese and scatter with snipped chives. Top the tortillas with the cooked mushrooms, 12 quartered cherry tomatoes, shredded lettuce, and 3 thinly sliced scallions. Roll up tightly, cut in half and serve.

Baked Mushroom Wraps in Hot Salsa Sauce Heat 1 tablespoon olive oil in a skillet over medium heat, then cook 1 lb large, flat field mushrooms, thickly sliced, with 2 finely chopped garlic cloves for 5–6 minutes until tender. Spread 4 low-fat or multiseed soft tortilla wrap breads with ½ cup extra-light cream cheese and spoon over the cooked mushrooms and 12 quartered cherry tomatoes. Roll up and place in an ovenproof dish in a single layer. Pour over a 10 oz jar chunky tomato salsa and scatter with 3 thinly sliced scallions and 2 tablespoons sliced jalapeños in brine. Bake in a preheated oven at 400°F for 15–18 minutes until hot. Meanwhile, mix together 6 tablespoons low-fat sour cream, 2 tablespoons lime juice, and 2 tablespoons snipped chives in a small bowl. Season with salt and pepper. Dress 2 shredded romaine lettuce hearts in the dressing and arrange on serving plates with the wraps to serve.

LOW-LIGH-WEL

3⬤ Butternut Squash and Ricotta Frittata

Serves 4

1 tablespoon canola oil
1 red onion, thinly sliced
1lb peeled butternut
   squash, diced
8 eggs
1 tablespoon snipped thyme
2 tablespoons chopped sage
½ cup ricotta
salt and pepper

- Heat the oil in a large, deep ovenproof skillet over medium-low heat, then add the onion and butternut squash. Cover loosely and cook gently, stirring frequently, for 18–20 minutes or until softened and golden.

- Beat the eggs lightly with the thyme, sage, and ricotta, then season generously with salt and pepper and pour over the butternut squash.

- Cook for a further 2–3 minutes until the egg is almost set, stirring occasionally with a heat-resistant rubber spatula to prevent the base from burning.

- Slide the pan under a preheated broiler and broil for 3–4 minutes, or until the egg is set and the frittata is golden. Slice into wedges and serve with a baby leaf salad.

1⬤ Strawberry and Ricotta Crêpes

Beat 4 tablespoons strawberry jam with 1 cup ricotta. Warm 8 ready-made crêpes, according to the package instructions, spread the ricotta mixture over the crêpes, then roll up loosely and place in an ovenproof dish. Dust with 1 tablespoon vanilla sugar and slide under a preheated hot broiler for 2–3 minutes until warm. Serve immediately with 1¼ cups sliced strawberries.

2⬤ Zucchini and Pea Frittata

 Heat 1 tablespoon canola oil in a skillet over medium heat, then add 1 thinly sliced red onion and stir-fry for 1 minute. Add 2 diced zucchini and cook for a further 4–5 minutes until softened, then stir in 1 cup frozen petit pois and cook for 1–2 minutes until thawed. Meanwhile, beat the eggs lightly with 2 tablespoons chopped mint, then add 7 oz cubed low-fat feta. Season generously with salt and pepper. Pour the egg mixture over the zucchini and peas and cook for 2–3 minutes, stirring occasionally. Slide under a preheated hot broiler for 2–3 minutes or until the eggs are set and golden. Serve in wedges with a baby leaf salad.

10 Fava Bean and Mint Hummus with Wholegrain Crostini

Serves 4

1¾ cups frozen peas

1¾ cups frozen baby fava beans, preferably peeled

1 wholegrain or granary baguette, sliced

½ cup fat-free Greek-style yogurt

2 tablespoons lemon juice

2 tablespoons chopped mint

salt and pepper

toasted sesame seeds, to garnish

- Put the peas and beans in a bowl and pour over enough boiling water to cover completely. Cover with a plate and set aside for 3 minutes. Drain and quickly cool under running cold water.

- Meanwhile, place the slices of wholegrain baguette under a preheated broiler to toast for 1–2 minutes each side until golden brown.

- Place the peas and beans in a food processor or blender. Add the yogurt, lemon juice, and 1 tablespoon of the mint. Blend until almost smooth. Scrape into a bowl and stir through the remaining mint, then season with salt and pepper.

- Spoon the pea and mint hummus into small bowls, scatter over toasted sesame seeds, and serve with the toasted baguette slices.

---

20 Warm Pea and Fava Bean Salad

with New Potatoes Cook 1 lb new potatoes in boiling water for 15–18 minutes until tender. Meanwhile, bring a saucepan of water to a boil and cook 1¾ cups each peas and beans for 3–4 minutes until tender. Drain and place in a large bowl with 2 finely sliced scallions, 2 tablespoons chopped mint, 2 tablespoons lemon juice, 2 tablespoons olive oil, 1½ cups chopped, ready-to-eat slow roasted tomatoes (not in oil) and salt and pepper. Tip in the potatoes, toss gently, and serve warm.

30 Baby Fava Bean and Pea Tart

Cook 1 cup each of frozen baby fava beans and frozen peas in boiling water for 3–4 minutes until tender. Cool under running cold water, drain well, and set aside. Place a 12 oz sheet of ready-rolled puff pastry on a cookie sheet and use a sharp knife to score a 1 inch border around the edge. Spread ⅔ cup low-fat cream cheese with chives over the pastry, keeping within the border. Scatter over the beans, the peas, and 2 finely sliced scallions. Season generously with salt and pepper

then crumble 1 cup low-fat feta cheese over the top. Cook in a preheated oven at 400°F for 20 minutes, or until golden. Serve in slices with mixed salad greens.

3O Warm Rainbow Salad with New Potatoes and Walnut Dressing

Serves 4

10 oz baby new potatoes
1 red pepper, seeded and sliced
1 yellow pepper, seeded and
  sliced
1 tablespoon olive oil
3 sprigs fresh thyme
1 large raw beet, peeled and
  coarsely grated
1 large carrot, coarsely grated
5 oz colorful mixed
  salad greens
2 tablespoons crushed walnuts
  (optional)
salt and pepper

Dressing

2 tablespoons walnut oil
1 tablespoon shallot vinegar
1 tablespoon Dijon mustard
pinch of sugar

- Preheat the oven to 375°F. Toss the potatoes and peppers in the olive oil with the thyme sprigs and season with plenty of salt and pepper. Tip into a large roasting pan and place in the oven for 20–25 minutes until tender. Meanwhile, combine the beet and carrot with the salad greens and divide among 4 serving plates.

- To make the dressing, put all the ingredients, along with a pinch of salt and pepper, into a jar with a tight-fitting lid. Seal and shake well to combine.

- Remove the roasting pan from the oven and discard the thyme. Arrange the vegetables onto the plates on top of the salad greens and drizzle with the dressing. Scatter over the walnuts, if using, and serve immediately.

1O Quick Rainbow Salad with Walnut

Dressing Make the dressing, as above. Arrange 5 oz colorful mixed salad greens on 4 serving plates and scatter over 1 thinly sliced red pepper and 1 thinly sliced yellow pepper. Coarsely grate 1 peeled beet, 1 carrot, and 1 yellow or green zucchini. Arrange over the salad greens and peppers then drizzle with the dressing. Scatter with 2 tablespoons crushed walnuts, if liked, and serve.

2O Rainbow Stir-Fry with Noodles

Cut 1 large peeled beet and 2 carrots into matchsticks, seed and thinly slice 1 red and 1 yellow pepper, and thickly slice 1 red onion. Cook 12 oz medium egg noodles according to the package instructions until "al dente" and drain in a colander. Heat 2 teaspoons sesame oil in a large wok or skillet over medium heat and stir-fry the onion for 30 seconds before adding the beet, carrots, and peppers. Stir-fry for 3–4 minutes until beginning to soften. Tip in the drained noodles and toss with the vegetables, adding 1 cup sweet chile stir-fry sauce, if liked. Heap onto serving plates and scatter over 1 tablespoon golden sesame seeds to serve.

Butterflied Sardines with Beet Salsa

Serves 4

4 tablespoons finely chopped parsley

finely grated zest of 1 lemon

2 teaspoons lemon juice

1 teaspoon harissa

2 garlic cloves, finely chopped

1 tablespoon canola oil

8–12 scaled and butterflied sardines (you can ask your fishmonger to do this for you)

2 tablespoons snipped dill

salt and cracked black pepper

Beet salsa

11½ oz cooked beet (not in vinegar), diced

½ red onion, very finely chopped

1 tablespoon aged sherry vinegar

2 tablespoons baby capers, rinsed and drained

- Mix together 2 tablespoons of the parsley, the lemon zest and juice, the harissa, garlic, and oil. Season with cracked black pepper, then rub the marinade over the sardines and set aside.

- To make the beet salsa mix together all the ingredients and season with salt and pepper.

- Lay the sardines on the rack of a broiler pan and slide under a preheated broiler for 2–3 minutes, turning once, or until cooked through.

- Arrange the sardines on serving plates with the beet salsa and scattered with the dill. Serve with toasted slices of ciabatta on the side.

Sardine, Chickpea, and Beet Salad

Prepare the beet salsa as above, adding 13 oz can chickpeas, drained. Toss through 8 oz baby leaf and herb salad. Drain 2 x 4 oz cans sardines and scatter the sardines over the salad. Divide the salad between 4 serving plates and sprinkle with 2 tablespoons snipped dill.

Linguine with Sardines and Beet

Cook 13 oz linguine for 11 minutes until "al dente," or according to the package instructions. Meanwhile, mix together 2 tablespoons finely chopped parsley, finely grated zest of 1 lemon, 1 teaspoon harissa, 2 finely chopped garlic cloves, and 1 tablespoon canola oil. Place 16 fresh sardine fillets on a nonstick baking pan. Rub the marinade over the sardine fillets, then slide them under a preheated broiler for 2–3 minutes until cooked and slightly charred, turning once. Flake the sardines roughly into a bowl, add 7 oz finely diced cooked beetroot (not in vinegar), 2 tablespoons chopped parsley, 2 teaspoons lemon juice, 2 tablespoons baby capers, and 1 finely chopped red chile. Mix together. Drain the linguine and toss through the sardine mixture until well combined, then serve.

30 Semidried Tomato and Italian Bean Soup

Serves 4

1 tablespoon olive oil

1 large onion, chopped

4 garlic cloves, roughly chopped

2 celery sticks, trimmed and
roughly chopped

1 carrot, diced

13 oz can peeled cherry tomatoes

8 ready-to-eat slow-roasted
tomatoes (not in oil), chopped

11½ oz can Tuscan bean mix or
13 oz can mixed beans, drained

1 tablespoon chopped oregano

3 cups vegetable stock

4 tablespoons ricotta

low-fat pesto or basil oil,
to drizzle (optional)

salt and pepper

- Heat the oil in a large, heavy-based pan over medium heat, then add the onion, garlic, celery, and carrots. Loosely cover and cook for 7–8 minutes, stirring occasionally, until softened and lightly colored.

- Add the cherry and slow-roasted tomatoes, beans, oregano, and stock. Bring to a boil. Reduce the heat slightly and simmer gently for 18 minutes, or until the vegetables are tender and the flavors have developed. Blend with a hand blender until smooth, then season with salt and pepper.

- Ladle the soup into bowls and serve topped with a spoonful of ricotta and a drizzle of pesto or basil oil, if liked, and crusty French bread.

 Italian Bean Salad

Mix together 11½ oz can Tuscan bean mix with 2 thinly sliced scallions, 8 chopped ready-to-eat slow-roasted tomatoes (not in oil), 2 thinly sliced celery sticks, and 1 coarsely grated carrot. Toss with 1 tablespoon low-fat pesto, 2 tablespoons lemon juice, and 4 oz arugula. Season generously with salt and pepper, then sprinkle over 2 tablespoons each of roughly chopped oregano and basil. Serve with crusty baguette.

 Quick Rustic Bean Soup

Heat 1 tablespoon olive oil in a large, heavy-based pan over medium heat, then add 1 chopped large onion and 4 roughly chopped garlic cloves. Cook for 4–5 minutes or until softened. Add 13 oz can mixed beans, drained, 2 tablespoons sun-dried tomato paste, 13 oz can peeled cherry tomatoes, 3 cups vegetable stock, and 1 tablespoon chopped oregano. Bring to a boil, then reduce the heat and simmer for 12–14 minutes until hot and fragrant. Ladle the soup into serving bowls and top each bowl with a spoonful of ricotta and a drizzle of low-fat pesto.

10 Quick Mushroom and Brown Rice Bowl

Serves 4

1 tablespoon olive oil

8 portabellini or small flat field mushrooms, chopped

1 teaspoon chopped tarragon

12½ oz cooked roast chicken slices, roughly chopped

2½ cups steamed brown basmati rice

4 oz lamb's lettuce or watercress

1 tablespoon Worcestershire sauce

Tabasco sauce, to taste (optional)

- Heat the olive oil in a large skillet over medium heat, then add the mushrooms and cook for 6–7 minutes, stirring frequently, until softened and golden. Stir in the chopped tarragon, chicken, and rice. Stir to heat through.

- Spoon the rice into serving bowls, scatter over the lamb's lettuce or watercress, and drizzle over the Worcestershire sauce. Sprinkle over a little Tabasco, if using, and serve immediately.

20 Grilled Mushroom Breakfast Bowl

Place 8 whole portabellini or small flat field mushrooms on a cookie sheet, stalk-side up. Scatter over 2 finely chopped garlic cloves and drizzle over 1 tablespoon olive oil. Slide the tray under a preheated broiler and cook for 7–8 minutes until tender. Meanwhile, cook 8 oz fine green beans in boiling water for 2–3 minutes until just tender, then drain. Heat 2½ cups steamed brown basmati rice. Thickly slice the grilled mushrooms, halve 16 cherry tomatoes, and cut the beans into 1½ inch lengths. Fold the vegetables into the rice with 1 teaspoon chopped tarragon. Season generously with salt and pepper and sprinkle over a dash of Worcestershire sauce and a dash of Tabasco sauce, if liked. Serve with lamb's lettuce.

30 Fragrant Brown Rice and Mushroom

Pilau Heat 2 tablespoons peanut oil in a skillet over medium heat. Add 1 finely chopped onion and 2 finely chopped garlic cloves. Cook for 5–6 minutes until softened. Add 8 chopped whole portabellini or small flat field mushrooms and cook for 2–3 minutes. Add ¼ teaspoon each of ground cardamom and ground cloves, ½ teaspoon ground cinnamon, 1 teaspoon ground cumin, and a generous pinch of saffron threads. Stir in 1 cup brown basmati rice and add 2¾ cups hot vegetable stock. Simmer gently for 15 minutes, turn off the heat, cover, and leave for 5 minutes or until the liquid is absorbed and the rice is tender.

30 Caper and Chorizo Stuffed Chicken Breast with Lima Beans

Serves 4

4 free-range chicken breasts, each about 5 oz

1 tablespoon capers, rinsed and drained

6 oz roasted red peppers from a jar, drained

8 thin slices lean chorizo

4 oz low-fat mozzarella, sliced

2 tablespoons chopped flat-leaf parsley

1 tablespoon olive oil

¾ cup dry white wine

2 x 13 oz cans lima beans, drained

1 cup ready-to-eat, slow-roasted tomatoes (not in oil), chopped

1 small red onion, finely chopped

3½ oz arugula

salt and pepper

- Cut the chicken breasts almost in half lengthways so that they open into a butterfly shape. Layer the capers, peppers, chorizo, and mozzarella over one side of each breast. Sprinkle with parsley and season with salt and pepper. Fold the other side of the breast over the filling, securing with a toothpick if necessary.

- Heat the oil in a large, nonstick skillet over medium heat. Add the chicken breasts and cook for 2–3 minutes each side until golden. Pour in the white wine and let it bubble gently for 5–6 minutes, or until the chicken is cooked through. Remove from the heat, cover, and set aside to rest.

- Meanwhile, toss the lima beans with the slow-roasted tomatoes, red onion, and arugula. Season with salt and pepper, then arrange on serving plates. Cut the chicken in half diagonally and arrange over the bean salad. Serve drizzled with the juices from the pan.

---

1 Chorizo and Lima Bean Salad

Mix together 6 oz roasted red peppers from a jar, drained, 2 x 13 oz cans lima beans, drained, 1 finely sliced small red onion, 1 cup chopped ready-to-eat, slow-roasted tomatoes (not in oil), 4 tablespoons chopped parsley, and 2 oz roughly chopped chorizo slices. Toss through 3½ oz arugula leaves, 1 tablespoon olive oil, and 2 tablespoons lemon juice. Season with salt and pepper and serve.

2 Toasted Spicy Chicken, Chorizo, and Mozzarella Panini

Split 4 part-baked baguettes in half lengthways and spread each base with a ½ teaspoon mild harissa paste. Divide 5 oz flame-grilled chicken slices, 2 oz thinly sliced, lean chorizo, ½ thinly sliced red onion, and 4 oz sliced low-fat mozzarella among the baguettes. Add 3½ oz arugula and 2 tablespoons chopped parsley and toast in a panini machine for 3–4 minutes until hot and melted. Alternatively, toast in a nonstick skillet over medium-high heat, placing another pan on top of the panini as a weight to hold them down. Toast for 2–3 minutes each side until hot and melting. Cut in half and serve.

LOW-LIGH-PAD

Great Chilled Gazpacho

Serves 4

1 lb 10 oz very red, ripe plum tomatoes, roughly chopped

1 small green pepper, cored, seeded, and chopped

1 small red pepper, cored, seeded, and chopped

½ small red onion, chopped

1 garlic clove, finely chopped

½ seeded cucumber, chopped

1¼ cups fresh bread crumbs

2 tablespoons olive oil

⅔ cup chilled tomato juice

2 tablespoons aged sherry vinegar

12 ice cubes

salt and pepper

1 tablespoon chopped mint, to garnish

- Put all the ingredients except the sherry vinegar, ice cubes, and mint into a food processor or blender and pulse until smooth. Stir in the vinegar and season generously with salt and pepper. Cover with plastic wrap and place in the freezer to chill for 10 minutes.

- Place 3 ice cubes in each serving bowl and pour over the chilled soup. Garnish with the chopped mint and serve.

Virgin Bloody Mary
Mix together in a large jug 2 cups tomato juice, 2 teaspoons lemon juice, 1 teaspoon celery salt, ½ teaspoon grated horseradish (optional), and a few shakes each of Tabasco and Worcestershire sauce, to taste. Add a few grinds of black pepper and pour into tall glasses filled with crushed ice. Garnish each with a trimmed celery stick and serve immediately.

Lemony Tomato and Pepper Pasta
Heat 1 tablespoon olive oil in a large, nonstick skillet over medium heat. Add 1 chopped red onion, 1 small seeded and chopped green pepper, and 1 small seeded and chopped red pepper. Cook, stirring occasionally, for 7–8 minutes until softened. Add 2 finely chopped garlic cloves and cook for a further 2 minutes.

Add 2 x 13 oz cans peeled cherry tomatoes, a pinch of sugar, 1 teaspoon finely grated lemon zest, 2 tablespoons sun-dried tomato puree, and ½ teaspoon each of dried red pepper flakes and dried oregano. Bring to a boil, reduce the heat to low, and simmer gently for 15–18 minutes until fragrant and heated through. Season with salt and pepper and serve tossed through 1 lb cooked pasta of your choice.

30 Hot Smoked Trout and Potato Salad

Serves 4

1 lb new potatoes
1 tablespoon olive oil
3 cups sugar snap peas, trimmed
and shredded
8 oz hot smoked trout fillets,
flaked
salt and cracked black pepper
lemon wedges, to serve (optional)

Dressing

1 tablespoon horseradish sauce
4 tablespoons low-fat crème
fraîche
1 tablespoon red wine vinegar
1 tablespoon chopped cocktail
gherkins or cornichons
1 scallion, sliced
2 tablespoons snipped chives

- Bring a large saucepan of lightly salted water to a boil and cook the new potatoes for 15–18 minutes, or until tender.

- Meanwhile, make the dressing. Mix together all the ingredients and season with cracked black pepper.

- Drain the potatoes, then pat dry and toss with the olive oil and a little salt and pepper. Tip into a large, nonstick skillet over medium-high heat, and fry for 4–5 minutes, turning frequently, or until golden and crisp.

- Tip the potatoes onto a plate lined with paper towels to remove any excess oil, then toss with the sugar snap peas. Arrange on serving plates topped with the smoked trout. Drizzle over the dressing, and serve immediately with lemon wedges, if liked, and sliced brown bread on the side.

---

1 Hot Smoked Trout Pâté Mash 8 oz flaked hot smoked trout fillets with the dressing ingredients as above and season with salt and pepper. Cut ½ seeded cucumber and 2 celery sticks into batons and toast 4 slices brown bread, then cut diagonally into quarters. To serve, arrange the trout pâté on one large plate or individual plates with the cucumber, celery, pieces of toast, and lemon wedges.

2 Smoked Trout Salad with Sweet Chile Dressing Cook 1 lb baby new potatoes in lightly salted water for 12–15 minutes until tender. Drain and cool under running cold water. Meanwhile, toss together 8 oz flaked hot smoked trout fillets, 7 oz crunchy mixed salad greens, 3 cups trimmed and shredded sugar snap peas, and 2 finely sliced scallions. In a separate bowl mix together 4 tablespoons sweet chile dipping sauce, 1 tablespoon lime juice, and 2 tablespoons chopped cilantro. Arrange the potatoes on serving plates and top with the smoked trout salad. Drizzle over the dressing and serve immediately.

Lime and Ginger Coleslaw with 5-Spiced Shrimp

Serves 4

½ Chinese cabbage or pointed
   spring cabbage, thinly shredded
2 carrots, coarsely grated
2 cups bean sprouts
1 small bunch of cilantro, finely
   chopped
2 scallions, thinly sliced
1 tablespoon groundnut oil
8 oz peeled raw jumbo shrimp
2 teaspoons Chinese 5-spice
   powder
lime wedges, to serve

Dressing

2 teaspoons finely grated fresh
   ginger root
2 tablespoons lime juice
1 teaspoon palm sugar or soft
   light brown sugar
2 tablespoons light soy sauce
1 tablespoon peanut oil

- Toss together in a large bowl the cabbage, carrots, bean sprouts, cilantro, and scallions. Set aside.

- To make the dressing, mix together all the dressing ingredients in a small bowl and set aside.

- Mix the shrimp with the Chinese 5-spice powder until well coated and add the oil to a nonstick wok or skillet over medium-high heat. Add the shrimp and toss to cook for 2–3 minutes, or until the shrimp are pink and cooked through. Remove from the heat and drain the shrimp on paper towels to remove any excess oil.

- Toss the dressing with the vegetables and heap the coleslaw on serving plates. Scatter over the shrimp and serve with lime wedges.

---

1 **Lime and Ginger Shrimp Rice Salad**

Make the dressing as above. Toss together 13 oz cooked, peeled shrimp with 1 lb ready-cooked wild basmati rice, 2 grated carrots, and 2 cups bean sprouts, then drizzle over the dressing. Sprinkle with 1 small bunch finely chopped cilantro and serve immediately.

3 **5-Spice Shrimp Skewers** Cook 1¼ cups wild basmati rice in lightly salted water for 15–18 minutes until tender, or according to the package instructions, then drain. Meanwhile, rub 1 tablespoon of Chinese 5-spice paste over 8 oz peeled raw jumbo shrimp and thread onto 4 metal skewers. Place the skewers on the rack over the broiler pan and slide under a preheated hot broiler for 3–4 minutes, turning occasionally, until cooked and slightly charred but still juicy. Prepare the coleslaw and dressing as above, halving the quantities. Arrange the shrimp skewers over the hot, drained rice and garnish with lime wedges. Serve with the coleslaw on the side.

30 Tomato and Bread Soup

Serves 4

4 thick slices slightly stale
sourdough bread, roughly
chopped

1 cup lowfat milk

2 lb very ripe plum tomatoes,
roughly chopped

4 garlic cloves, roughly chopped

1 large bunch of basil, leaves
stripped and roughly chopped

2 tablespoons olive oil

½ cucumber, seeded and finely
diced

½ small red onion, finely chopped

2 teaspoons capers, rinsed and
drained

2 teaspoons red wine vinegar

1½ cups vegetable stock

salt and pepper

- Preheat the oven to 400°F. Place the bread in a bowl, pour over the milk, and set aside.

- Tip the tomatoes into a large roasting pan. Add the garlic, all but 2 tablespoons of the basil and 1 tablespoon of the olive oil, and season generously with salt and pepper. Place in the oven for 20–25 minutes, or until collapsed and softened.

- Meanwhile, mix together the cucumber, red onion, capers, red wine vinegar, the remaining oil, and the 2 tablespoons reserved basil leaves. Season with salt and pepper and set aside.

- Pour the stock into a saucepan and bring to a boil. Squeeze the excess milk from the soaked bread.

- Remove the tomatoes from the oven, stir in the squeezed, soaked bread and enough hot vegetable stock to give the soup a thick, rich texture. Ladle the soup into serving bowls, top each bowl with a spoonful of the cucumber salsa, and serve.

---

1 Summery Bruschetta with Tomatoes

Toast 4 large slices of sourdough bread on a ridged griddle pan until charred, then rub with the cut edges of 1 garlic clove. Mix together 2 lb roughly chopped ripe plum tomatoes, ½ seeded and finely chopped cucumber, ½ finely chopped red onion, 2 teaspoons rinsed and drained capers, 2 teaspoons red wine vinegar, 2 tablespoons olive oil, and roughly chopped leaves from 1 large bunch of basil. Spoon onto the garlicky toast and serve immediately.

2 "Panzanella" Tomato and Bread Salad

Lightly toast 4 thick slices of slightly stale sourdough bread and cut into cubes. Mix together 2 lb roughly chopped very ripe plum tomatoes, the roughly chopped leaves from 1 large bunch of basil, ½ finely chopped small red onion, 2 teaspoons rinsed and drained capers, 2 tablespoons olive oil, and 2 teaspoons red wine vinegar. Season generously with salt and pepper, then stir in the cubes of toast and set aside for 10–15 minutes for the bread to

absorb the juices. Serve with an extra drizzle of olive oil, if desired.

20 Smoked Chicken with Beans, Walnuts, and Tarragon

Serves 4

7 oz fine green beans, trimmed

1 firm, ripe Hass avocado, pitted and peeled

1 tablespoon lemon juice

7 oz mesclun or mixed leaf salad

10 oz cooked whole smoked chicken breasts, roughly chopped

1 yellow pepper, finely chopped

½ cup walnut pieces

1 shallot, finely chopped (optional)

2 teaspoons chopped tarragon

4 teaspoons walnut oil

salt and pepper

lemon wedges, to serve

- Bring a small saucepan of lightly salted water to a boil. When the water is boiling add the beans and cook for 3–4 minutes until just tender, then drain the beans and cool them under running cold water.

- Meanwhile, dice the flesh of the avocado and toss in the lemon juice to prevent it from turning brown.

- Place the mesclun or mixed leaf salad in a large bowl. Add the chicken, pepper, walnuts, beans, and avocado, then gently toss until well combined.

- Heap the salad onto serving plates and sprinkle over the shallot, if using, and tarragon. Season with a little salt and plenty of pepper, then drizzle over the walnut oil. Serve immediately with lemon wedges and nutty granary bread on the side.

 Healthy Chicken and Avocado Baguettes

Mash the flesh from 1 ripe avocado with 1 tablespoon lemon juice and plenty of black pepper, then spread over the base of 4 small, granary baguettes. Slice 10 oz cooked whole smoked chicken breasts and layer on top of the avocado. Scatter over 4 teaspoons chopped walnut pieces, 1 finely chopped shallot, and 2 teaspoons chopped tarragon, then finish with 7 oz mesclun or mixed leaf salad. Drizzle over a little walnut oil and lemon juice, if liked. Cut in half and serve.

 Ricotta and Tarragon Chicken Parcels

Using a sharp knife, cut deep slits along the sides of 4 skinless chicken breasts, about 5 oz each, to create 4 pockets. Mix together ½ cup ricotta, ¼ cup chopped walnuts, 2 teaspoons tarragon, and 1 finely sliced shallot. Season with salt and pepper. Spoon the ricotta mixture into the pockets, then wrap each breast in a large slice of Parma ham. Heat 1 tablespoon olive oil in a nonstick skillet over a medium–high heat and fry for 4–5 minutes each side until almost cooked through. Add ½ cup dry white wine to the pan and simmer for 2–3 minutes or until the chicken is cooked. Meanwhile, cook 7 oz trimmed fine green beans in boiling water for 3–4 minutes or until just tender. Cool under running cold water. Remove the chicken from the heat and cut into thick slices. To assemble, arrange the chicken over the cooked green beans on serving plates. Serve with a mesclun salad dressed in walnut oil, if liked, and lemon wedges.

LOW-LIGH-GEH

10 Real Guacamole with Raw Vegetables

Serves 4

2 large, firm, ripe avocados
½ small red onion
2 tablespoons lime juice
3 tablespoons finely chopped
  cilantro
¼ teaspoon garlic powder
¼ teaspoon celery salt
pinch of cayenne
½ teaspoon paprika
3 tomatoes
few dashes of Tabasco (optional)
salt and pepper

To serve

11½ oz carrots, cut into batons
1½ cups cauliflower florets
4 celery sticks, cut into batons
8 oz radishes, trimmed
4 oz baby sweetcorn

- Peel the avocados and remove the pits, then mash the flesh in a small bowl with the back of a fork or potato masher to break it up.

- Finely chop the red onion and add to the avocado along with the lime juice, cilantro, garlic powder, celery salt, and spices. Mix until almost smooth, with some small lumps, then season with salt and pepper.

- Quarter, seed, and finely chop the tomatoes, then stir them into the avocado mixture. Add the Tabasco, if using.

- Scoop into a serving bowl and arrange on a platter with the selection of raw vegetables.

 Avocado and Crabmeat Salad

Combine together in a bowl 10 oz cooked white crabmeat, the finely grated zest and juice of 1 lime, 1 finely chopped shallot, 3 tablespoons chopped cilantro, 1 seeded and finely chopped red chile, and ½ small seeded and finely chopped cucumber. Cut 2 large, firm, ripe avocados in half and remove the pits. Spoon the crab salad into the avocado halves and serve with slices of lightly buttered brown bread.

 Steak Wraps with Chunky Guacamole

Rub a 13 oz lean rump steak with 1 tablespoon olive oil and 1 tablespoon spicy Cajun seasoning mix. Heat a ridged griddle pan over medium–high heat and cook the steak, turning occasionally, for 4–5 minutes or until nicely charred and almost cooked but still pink. Remove the steak from the heat and set aside to rest. Meanwhile, dice the flesh of 2 large, firm, ripe avocados and toss gently with the guacamole ingredients, as above. Scatter 4 large, warmed multiseed bread wraps with ½ shredded iceberg lettuce and 1 seeded and thinly sliced red pepper. Slice the steak thinly and arrange over the salad. Spoon over the guacamole, then roll up the wraps tightly. Cut in half and serve immediately with a few dashes of Tabasco sprinkled over, if liked.

Mixed Rice and Bean Salad with Smoked Duck Breast

Serves 4

1 scant cup basmati and wild rice mix, rinsed in cold water

1 green pepper, cored, seeded, and diced

1 small mango, peeled, seeded, and diced

1 large bunch of cilantro

2 scallions, finely sliced (optional)

13 oz can azuki beans, drained

4 tablespoons lime juice

11½ oz smoked duck breast, trimmed of excess fat and sliced

handful of alfalfa shoots

salt and pepper

lime wedges, to serve

- Bring 2 cups lightly salted water to a boil, tip in the rice, and cook for 15–18 minutes until the rice is tender, or according to the package instructions. Drain into a sieve and cool quickly under cold running water.

- Meanwhile, mix together the pepper, mango, cilantro, scallions, if using, azuki beans, and lime juice in a large bowl.

- Fold the cooled rice into the azuki bean salad and divide into deep serving bowls. Arrange the slices of duck breast over the salad, then top with the alfalfa sprouts. Serve immediately with lime wedges on the side.

 Quick Bean, Rice, and Tuna Salad

Mix together in a large bowl 2¾ cups cooked wild and basmati rice, 1 seeded and diced green pepper, 1 small diced cucumber, 1 chopped large bunch cilantro, 13 oz can azuki beans, drained, 4 tablespoons lime juice, and 2 finely sliced scallions, if liked. Season with salt and pepper, then divide into serving bowls. Top with 11½ oz flaked smoked tuna, and serve.

Pan-Fried Duck Breast with Azuki Rice Mix and Mango Salsa

Cook 1 scant cup basmati and wild rice mix in 2 cups lightly salted water for 15–18 minutes until the rice is tender, or according to the package instructions. Meanwhile, make a salsa by mixing together 1 seeded and diced yellow pepper, the diced flesh of 1 mango, 1 chopped large bunch of cilantro, and 2 finely sliced scallions. Stir in 2 tablespoons lime juice and 1 tablespoon vegetable oil. Set aside. Heat 1 tablespoon of vegetable oil in a large, nonstick skillet over medium-high heat and fry 14½ oz duck mini fillets for 4–6 minutes until cooked, turning occasionally. Remove from the heat and set aside to rest for 2–3 minutes. Tip a 13 oz can azuki beans into a sieve and drain the cooked rice directly over the beans to heat them. Drain well, then spoon onto serving plates. Cut the duck fillets into slices and arrange them over the bean and rice mix. Serve immediately with the salsa and lime wedges on the side.

10 Roasted Peppers on Rye

Serves 4

8 slices seeded rye bread or
   multigrain bread
1 garlic clove, halved (optional)
6 oz flame-roasted red peppers,
   drained and sliced
2 tablespoons toasted pine nuts
3½ oz low-fat feta cheese
   (optional)

Artichoke paste

13 oz can artichokes in water,
   drained
4 oz ricotta or extra-light cream
   cheese
1 tablespoon lemon juice
salt and pepper

- Heat a ridged griddle pan over high heat and toast the sliced bread for 1–2 minutes each side until toasted and lightly charred. Rub the toast with the cut edges of the garlic clove, if liked.

- To make the artichoke paste, put the artichokes in the small bowl of a food processor or blender and pulse until roughly chopped and textured. Add the ricotta and lemon juice and pulse to a paste. Season with salt and pepper.

- Spread the artichoke paste over the slices of toast and top the paste with the roasted peppers. Sprinkle over the toasted pine nuts, crumble over the feta, if using, and serve.

---

20 Pepper, Artichoke, and Spinach Pizzas

Make the artichoke paste as above, and spread over 2 large ready-made pizza bases. Scatter over 3 cups baby leaf spinach and top with a 9 oz jar well-drained, mixed, sliced peppers. Crumble over 3½ oz low-fat feta cheese and sprinkle with 2 tablespoons toasted pine nuts. Place in a preheated oven at 425°F for 10–12 minutes until the pizzas are crisp.

30 Spicy Bulghur Wheat and Roast

Peppers Bring 2 cups vegetable stock to a boil in a large saucepan. Add 1½ cups bulghur wheat and cook for 7 minutes. Turn off the heat, cover, and leave for 12–15 minutes until the liquid is absorbed and the grains are tender. Meanwhile, fry 1 chopped red onion and 2 chopped garlic cloves in 1 tablespoon olive oil for 5–6 minutes until softened, stirring occasionally. Add 2¾ cups chopped mushrooms and cook for 2–3 minutes until tender, then add a 13 oz can artichokes in water, drained and roughly chopped, 6 oz chopped roasted peppers, 2 tablespoons lemon juice, and 1 small bunch of chopped cilantro. Fold through the bulghur wheat. Serve topped with dollops of fat-free Greek-style yogurt and lemon wedges for squeezing.

20 Fragrant Soba Noodle Soup

Serves 4

1 lemon grass stalk, leaves stripped

5 cups clear chicken or vegetable stock

1 inch piece of fresh ginger root, finely chopped

3 lime leaves, thinly sliced

1 small red chile, seeded and finely sliced (optional)

1 tablespoon fish sauce

8 oz buckwheat soba noodles

7 oz firm tofu, diced

1 scallion, thinly sliced

2 tablespoons chopped cilantro

- Finely slice the lemon grass stalk and place in a saucepan with the chicken stock, ginger root, lime leaves, chile, if using, and fish sauce. Bring to a boil, then reduce the heat to low and simmer gently for 10–12 minutes.

- Meanwhile, bring a large saucepan of water to a boil and cook the noodles for 6–7 minutes until tender, or according to the package instructions. Drain the noodles and divide among 4 warmed bowls.

- Scatter the tofu over the noodles and then carefully ladle over the hot, fragrant soup. Scatter over the scallions and cilantro, and serve immediately.

 ### Mixed Noodle and Chicken Thai Broth

Cook 8 oz buckwheat soba noodles as above, and heat 11 ½ oz cooked medium egg noodles according to the package instructions. Meanwhile, heat 5 cups chicken stock in a saucepan with 1 teaspoon each of minced lemon grass, fresh ginger root, and Thai red chile paste (nam prik pao). Simmer for 3–4 minutes. Divide the noodles between 4 deep bowls and scatter over 10 oz diced, cooked chicken. Ladle over the hot broth and serve with 1 sliced scallion and chopped cilantro.

 ### Chicken and Soba Noodle Salad

Cook 8 oz buckwheat soba noodles in boiling water or 5 cups clear chicken stock for 6–7 minutes or until tender. Drain and cool under cold running water. Meanwhile, put 1 lemon grass stalk, leaves stripped and roughly chopped, 1 inch peeled and finely chopped fresh ginger root, and 1 seeded and roughly chopped small red chile in a mini chopper. Add 2 tablespoons peanut oil and 4 tablespoons lime juice, then blend until smooth. Toss the cooked noodles in the lemon grass dressing and set aside.

Shred 13 oz cooked chicken into a separate bowl, then mix in 7 oz diced firm tofu and 1 ¼ cups shredded sugar snap peas. Tip in the dressed noodles and toss gently to combine. Pile the noodle salad on serving plates, scatter over 1 thinly sliced scallion, 2 tablespoons chopped cilantro, and 2 tablespoons chopped blanched peanuts. Serve immediately.

LOW-LIGH-HOR

QuickCook
Fish and Shellfish

Recipes listed by cooking time

10

Pan-Fried Salmon with Mixed Bean Salad

Serves 4

1 tablespoon canola oil
4 tail-end salmon fillets, about
  5 oz each
cracked black pepper

Mixed bean salad

2 x 13 oz cans mixed beans,
  drained
½ tablespoon canola oil
1 tablespoon red wine vinegar
2 tablespoons finely chopped
  mint
3 oz arugula
salt

- Heat the oil in a large, nonstick skillet over medium heat. Season the salmon fillets with cracked black pepper, then place them skin-side down in the pan and fry for 2–3 minutes until golden and crispy. Turn the fillets over and fry for a further 2–3 minutes until almost cooked.

- Meanwhile, to make the mixed bean salad, put the mixed beans, the oil, vinegar, and mint in a large bowl and mix to combine. Season with salt and pepper, then toss through the arugula.

- Transfer the mixed bean salad to serving plates, top with the salmon fillets, and serve.

---

2 Baked Salmon and Mixed Beans

Prepare the mixed bean salad as above, omitting the arugula. Divide the bean salad among 4 large pieces of parchment paper and top each mound of beans with a tail-end salmon fillet, about 5 oz each. Fold the edges of the paper over the beans and salmon to make 4 sealed parcels. Place the parcels on a large cookie sheet and put in a preheated oven at 400°F for 12–15 minutes or until the fish is cooked and the beans are hot. Serve with arugula.

3 Salmon, Bean, and Couscous Salad

Season 4 chunky salmon fillets, about 5 oz each, with cracked black pepper. Heat 1 tablespoon canola oil over medium heat. Add the the fillets and fry for 7–8 minutes, or until cooked through, turning once. Set aside to cool, then flake the fillets into large pieces. Pour 1 cup boiling water over ¾ cup lemon and cilantro couscous and leave to stand for 5 minutes until the liquid is absorbed and the grains are tender. Add to the couscous a 13 oz can mixed beans, drained,

2 tablespoons chopped mint, 2 sliced scallions, 2 tablespoons lemon juice, and ½ tablespoon canola oil. Season generously with salt and pepper. Bring a small saucepan of water to a boil and cook 7 oz trimmed asparagus tips for 2–3 minutes until just tender. Drain and cool under cold running water. Toss the asparagus with the mixed bean and couscous salad. Serve topped with the flaked salmon.

30 Hot and Sour Shrimp Soup

Serves 4

4 cups light and clear chicken or vegetable stock

3 tablespoons Thai fish sauce

1 tablespoon rice wine vinegar

1 tablespoon lime juice

1 tablespoon palm sugar or soft light brown sugar

1 garlic clove, sliced

1 red chile, sliced thinly

3 lime leaves

2 teaspoons tamarind paste

7 oz rice vermicelli

4 oz baby corn, sliced

8 oz raw peeled jumbo shrimp

1 cup bean sprouts

2 tablespoons shredded mint

- Pour the stock into a large saucepan and add the fish sauce, vinegar, lime juice, sugar, garlic, chile, lime leaves, and tamarind paste. Bring to a boil over medium-high heat, then reduce the heat and simmer gently for 12 minutes.

- Meanwhile, put the rice vermicelli in a bowl of boiling water for 2–3 minutes until tender, or cook according to the package instructions. Drain well and divide among warmed deep serving bowls.

- Stir the baby corn into the broth and simmer for 2 minutes, then add the shrimp and simmer for a further 2–3 minutes, or until the shrimp are just cooked.

- Ladle the broth into the bowls of vermicelli, then scatter over the bean sprouts and mint, and serve immediately

1 Thai Shrimp and Coconut Soup

Bring 2 cups chicken stock to a boil. Stir in 4 tablespoons Thai tom yum paste, 2 tablespoons lime juice, 3 fresh lime leaves, and 1 teaspoon fish sauce. Reduce the heat and simmer for 4–5 minutes. Cook 7 oz rice vermicelli as above, then divide among 4 deep bowls. Stir 4 oz sliced baby corn and 8 oz raw peeled jumbo shrimp into the soup and simmer for 2–3 minutes until the shrimp are cooked. Add ¾ cup low-fat coconut milk and bring to a boil. Ladle over the vermicelli and serve.

2 Hot and Sour Shrimp Stir-Fry

Mix together in a small bowl 2 tablespoons fish sauce, 1 tablespoon each of rice wine vinegar and lime juice, 1 tablespoon palm sugar or soft light brown sugar, and 2 teaspoons tamarind paste. Heat 1 tablespoon peanut oil in a hot wok over medium-high heat and stir-fry 2 sliced garlic cloves, 1 thinly sliced red chile (remove seeds for less heat), 1 tablespoon chopped fresh ginger root, and 1 sliced shallot for 30 seconds. Tip in 8 oz raw peeled jumbo shrimp and stir-fry for 2–3 minutes until just cooked through. Turn off the heat, pour over the dressing mixture, and set aside to cool. Meanwhile, cook 7 oz rice vermicelli as above, then cool in ice-cold water. When ready to serve, drain the vermicelli and toss with the cooled shrimp mixture, 1 cup bean sprouts, and 2 tablespoons shredded mint. Serve with lime wedges on the side.

Grilled Sardines with Mango and Lime Salsa

Serves 4

1 teaspoon finely grated fresh ginger root

finely grated zest and juice of 1 lime

1 small bunch of cilantro, roughly chopped

1 tablespoon peanut oil

½ large red chile, seeded and chopped

12–16 fresh sardines, scaled, gutted, and cleaned

Mango and lime salsa

1 firm, ripe mango, peeled, seeded, and diced

4 tomatoes, seeded and diced

1 scallion, finely chopped

2 tablespoons lime juice

½ large red chile, seeded and chopped

- Place the ginger root, lime zest and juice, cilantro, oil, and half the chile in a mini chopper and blend to make a rough paste. Alternatively, use a mortar and pestle.

- Score small slits into the sardine flesh, then rub the paste all over, massaging it into the slits.

- Place the sardines onto a wire rack over a broiler pan and slide under a hot preheated broiler for 4–5 minutes, or until cooked and slightly blackened, turning once.

- Meanwhile, make the salsa by combining all the ingredients in a small bowl and mixing well.

- Serve the sardines straight off the grill with the salsa.

 Sardines on Toast with Mango and Lime Salsa Make the salsa as above and grill 4 large slices of bread. Arrange 10 oz canned sardines in hot chile or piri-piri on the toasted bread and serve with the salsa.

 Grilled Sardines with Cumin Potatoes and Mango and Lime Salsa Tip 1 lb small new potatoes into a large saucepan with 1 tablespoon olive oil, some coarse sea salt, and 1–2 teaspoon cumin seeds, to taste. Cook for 20–25 minutes, shaking the pan frequently, until golden and crisp. Meanwhile, place 1 teaspoon finely grated fresh ginger root, the finely grated zest and juice of 1 lime, 1 small roughly chopped bunch of cilantro, 1 tablespoon peanut oil, and ½ large seeded and chopped red chile in a mini chopper or mortar and pestle. Grind to a rough paste. Rub the prepared paste all over 12–16 scaled, gutted, and cleaned fresh sardines. Set them on a broiler rack under a preheated broiler for 8–10 minutes until golden and cooked, turning once. Serve with the cumin potatoes and the mango and lime salsa, as above.

10 Spicy Seafood Salad

Serves 4

1 teaspoon superfine sugar

2 tablespoons mirin

1 tablespoon light soy sauce

1 small red chile, seeded and finely chopped

2 tablespoons lime juice

11½ oz fine egg noodles

13 oz cooked fruits de mer or seafood selection

lime wedges, to serve

- Place the sugar, mirin, soy sauce, chile, and lime juice in a small saucepan over medium-low heat and stir until the sugar has dissolved. Pour the dressing into a jug or bowl and set aside for the flavors to develop.

- Meanwhile, cook the noodles in a large saucepan of boiling water for 2–3 minutes until tender, or according to the package instructions. Then cool under cold running water and drain well.

- Tip the fruits de mer or seafood selection into a large bowl. Add the noodles and dressing and toss until the seafood and noodles are well coated in the dressing. Serve immediately with lime wedges.

20 Chile Seafood Linguine

Cook 13 oz linguine in a saucepan of salted boiling water, according to the package instructions. Meanwhile, heat 1 tablespoon olive oil in a nonstick skillet over medium heat, and add 1 small seeded and chopped red chile, 2 finely chopped garlic cloves, and 2 finely sliced scallions. Cook gently for 2–3 minutes, then add 1¾ cups halved cherry tomatoes and 3 tablespoons lime juice. Season generously with salt and pepper, then tip in 13 oz cooked fruits de mer or seafood selection and stir-fry for 1 minute to reheat. Remove from the heat, tip in the drained linguine, and toss until well combined. Serve immediately.

30 Seafood Risotto

Pour 3¾ cups vegetable stock into a saucepan and bring up to a gentle boil. Meanwhile, heat 1 tablespoon olive oil in a large skillet over medium heat, add 2 chopped shallots, and cook for 4–5 minutes until softened. Add 1½ cups risotto rice and stir for a minute, or until the grains are well coated and look translucent. Add ⅓ cup dry vermouth, then simmer rapidly until absorbed, stirring constantly. Stirring and simmering constantly, take 17 minutes to incorporate the boiling vegetable stock, a ladleful at a time, or until the rice is "al dente." When the risotto is cooked, stir in 2 teaspoons grated lemon zest and 13 oz cooked fruits de mer or seafood selection. Season with salt and pepper and stir until the seafood is heated through. Spoon into deep bowls and serve.

Baked Sea Bream with Cumin and Cucumber Yogurt

Serves 4

2 garlic cloves, finely chopped

2 tablespoons chopped parsley

finely grated zest of 1 lemon

¼ teaspoon dried red pepper flakes (optional)

1 teaspoon cumin seeds, crushed

1 tablespoon olive oil

4 sea bream fillets, about 5 oz each, pin-boned

¼ cup dry white wine

lemon wedges, to serve

salt and pepper

Cumin and cucumber yogurt

1 teaspoon cumin seeds, crushed

½ small cucumber

6 tablespoons fat-free plain yogurt

2 teaspoons lemon juice

- Preheat the oven to 425°F. Mix together the garlic, parsley, lemon zest, dried red pepper flakes, and cumin seeds in a small bowl. Stir in the olive oil and then rub the mixture over the sea bream fillets.

- Put the fillets in a foil-lined roasting pan and pour over the white wine. Season with salt and pepper and cover with foil, sealing tightly. Place in the oven and bake for about 8 minutes, or until the fish is just cooked through.

- Meanwhile make the cumin and cucumber yogurt. Heat a small skillet over medium heat, then add the cumin seeds and dry roast until they begin to smell fragrant. Seed and finely chop the cucumber, tip into a bowl, mix with the yogurt and lemon juice, and season.

- Remove the sea bream from the oven and serve immediately drizzled with any juices from the roasting pan, alongside steamed basmati rice, the cumin and cucumber yogurt, and poppadums on the side.

 Sea Bream with Cumin-Scented Yogurt Pin-bone 4 sea bream fillets, 5 oz each, and season with salt and pepper. Add 1 tablespoon olive oil to a large skillet over medium heat. Add the fillets, skin-side down and fry for 3–4 minutes until crisp. Turn and fry for 2–3 more minutes until cooked through. Meanwhile, mix ½ teaspoon ground cumin, 6 tablespoons fat-free plain yogurt, 2 teaspoons lemon juice, and 2 tablespoons chopped parsley, and season. Serve with the fish and steamed rice.

Baked Sea Bream and Spinach Parcels Ask the fishmonger to fillet 4 small sea bream. Mix together 2 finely chopped garlic cloves, 2 tablespoons chopped parsley, the finely grated zest of 1 lemon, and 2 teaspoons cumin seeds with 7 oz baby leaf spinach in a large skillet over medium heat until the spinach is just wilted. Place 1 fillet from each sea bream on a foil-lined baking pan, skin-side down. Top each fillet with one-quarter of the wilted spinach, then cover with the corresponding fillet, skin-side up

this time, to form 4 parcels. Secure each parcel with toothpicks or tie with string. Bake in a preheated oven at 425°F for about 15 minutes, or until cooked through and the flesh flakes easily when pressed in the center with a knife. Serve with steamed brown basmati rice and the cumin and cucumber yogurt as above.

LOW-FISH-FEF

 Soy and Ginger Tuna Fishcakes

Serves 4

14½ oz tuna steak, roughly
 chopped
2 tablespoons sweet soy sauce
 (ketjap manis)
2 teaspoons finely grated fresh
 ginger root
1 long shallot, finely chopped
2 tablespoons beaten egg
1¾ cups panko or coarse, crisp
 bread crumbs
peanut oil, for greasing
sweet chile dipping sauce, to
 serve

Soy dipping sauce

2 tablespoons dark soy sauce
2 tablespoons mirin
2 tablespoons sake
2 teaspoons finely grated fresh
 ginger root

- Preheat the oven to 400°F. To make the soy dipping sauce, put all the ingredients in a small saucepan over medium-high heat and bring up to boiling point. Reduce the heat and simmer for 2–3 minutes, pour the sauce into a shallow serving dish, and set aside to cool.

- Meanwhile, place the tuna in the bowl of a food processor or blender with the sweet soy sauce (ketjap manis), ginger root, shallot, and egg. Pulse quickly to just combine, then stir in ¾ cup of the panko or bread crumbs. Form the mixture into 8 small fishcakes and coat each one well in the remaining bread crumbs.

- Place the fishcakes on a lightly greased, nonstick cookie sheet and bake in the oven for 15 minutes, or until crisp and golden, turning once.

- Once the fishcakes are cooked, arrange them on serving plates with the soy dipping sauce and sweet chile dipping sauce served separately.

 Quick Tuna Fishcakes

Mix a 13 oz can tuna in brine, drained, with 4 teaspoons finely grated ginger root, 2 beaten eggs, and ¾ cup panko or coarse, crisp bread crumbs. Form into 4 large, flattened fishcakes. Coat in another ¾ cup panko or coarse, crisp bread crumbs. Heat 1 tablespoon peanut oil in a skillet over medium heat, then fry the fishcakes for 4–5 minutes or until crisp, turning once. Serve with sweet chile dipping sauce on the side.

 Tuna Rösti
Coarsely grate 2 large potatoes and 2 carrots. Place in a sieve over the sink and squeeze out any excess moisture. Flake a 3½ oz can of tuna in brine, drained, into a large bowl and mix with 1 small, beaten egg, 2 tablespoons chopped cilantro, and the grated vegetables. Heat 1 tablespoon peanut oil in a large, nonstick skillet over medium heat, then scrape the tuna and potato mixture into the pan to make 1 large rösti. Cook for about 4 minutes or until crisp and

golden, then flip over and cook for a further 3–4 minutes. Carefully remove to a plate lined with paper towels to drain off any excess fat. Serve in wedges with the soy dipping sauce, as above, and sweet chile dipping sauce.

3⓪ Cajun-Spiced Jumbo Shrimp with Mixed Rice

Serves 4

1½ cups long-grain wild rice
13 oz raw peeled jumbo shrimp
1 large red pepper, thinly sliced
1 red onion, cut into thin wedges

Cajun spice mix

1 teaspoon cayenne pepper
1 teaspoon paprika
1 teaspoon dried thyme
1 teaspoon dried oregano
½ teaspoon dried onion granules
½ teaspoon dried garlic granules
½ teaspoon ground cumin
½ teaspoon sea salt
½ teaspoon black pepper

To serve

arugula
lime wedges
griddled flour tortillas (optional)

- Bring a large saucepan of salted water to a boil and cook the rice for 15–18 minutes, or according to the package instructions.

- Meanwhile, combine the Cajun spice mix ingredients in a large bowl, add the shrimp, and toss until well coated with the spices. Lay the pepper and onion on a small baking pan and place under a preheated broiler for 4–5 minutes until beginning to lightly char.

- Remove the pan from under the broiler and turn over the vegetables. Arrange the shrimp in a single layer on a separate small baking pan and place both pan under the broiler for a further 4–5 minutes, turning the shrimp once. The shrimp should be cooked through but still juicy and the peppers and onions should be slightly charred but still firm.

- Drain the rice thoroughly and spoon onto serving plates. Scatter the peppers and onions over the rice, arrange the shrimp on top, and serve immediately with a few arugula leaves, lime wedges, and griddled flour tortillas, if desired.

1⓪ Quick Spiced Shrimp Rice Salad

Take 1 lb ready-cooked rice, but do not heat. Tip the rice into a large bowl and add 1 thinly sliced red pepper and 1 red onion, cut into very thin wedges. In a separate bowl toss 13 oz cooked peeled jumbo shrimp with 1½ tablespoons ready-made Cajun seasoning. Heat 1 tablespoon vegetable oil in a skillet over high heat, add the shrimp, and fry for 1 minute to heat through. Scatter over the salad and serve.

2⓪ Quick Cajun Shrimp Rice

Heat 1 lb ready-cooked wild basmati rice according to the package instructions. Heat 1 tablespoon vegetable oil in a nonstick skillet over medium heat, then add 1 small, thinly sliced red onion and 1 seeded and thinly sliced pepper. Cook, stirring occasionally, for 6–7 minutes, or until softened and golden. Meanwhile, make the Cajun spice mix as above, then add 13 oz raw peeled jumbo shrimp and toss until the shrimp are well coated in the mix. Tip the shrimp into the pan with the vegetables for a further 3–4 minutes until the shrimp are pink and cooked through. Toss with the hot rice and serve in bowls with a few arugula leaves, lime wedges, and tortillas, as above.

Swordfish Steaks with Basil and Pine Nut Oil

Serves 4

1 teaspoon canola oil

4 swordfish steaks, about 5 oz each

8 oz herby baby leaf salad

1½ cups ready-to-eat, slow-roasted tomatoes (not in oil), roughly chopped

salt and pepper

Basil and pine nut oil

1 small bunch of basil, leaves stripped

5 teaspoons canola oil

1 tablespoon toasted pine nuts

1 tablespoon lemon juice

- Rub the oil over the swordfish steaks and season generously with salt and pepper. Place on a preheated ridged griddle pan over medium heat and cook for 5–7 minutes, turning once, until the fish is nicely charred but still slightly rare.

- Meanwhile, to make the basil oil, put all the ingredients in a mini chopper or in a small food processor and pulse to blend to a smooth paste. Season the basil oil with salt and pepper, then scrape into a small bowl. Alternatively, crush in a mortar and pestle.

- Pile the baby leaf salad onto serving plates and scatter with the slow-roasted tomatoes. Serve alongside the griddled swordfish, with a little basil and pine nut oil drizzled over each.

2 Griddled Swordfish with Basil-Dressed Warm Potato Salad Cook 11½ oz baby new potatoes in a saucepan of salted boiling water for 15–18 minutes until tender. Meanwhile, make the basil and pine nut oil as above, and griddle 4 swordfish steaks, about 5 oz each, as above. While the swordfish is grilling, cook 7 oz green beans for 3–4 minutes until tender but still firm, then drain and place in a bowl with 1½ cups roughly chopped ready-to-eat, slow-roasted tomatoes (not in oil), 2 sliced scallions, and ½ cup pitted black olives. Slice the swordfish steaks thickly. Drain the potatoes and toss with the tomatoes and beans and half of the basil and pine nut oil. Transfer the vegetables to serving plates, then top with the swordfish. Serve drizzled with the remaining basil and pine nut oil.

3 Pan-Fried Tuna Marinated in Basil-Infused Oil Put the leaves from 1 small bunch of basil and 5 teaspoons canola oil into a mini chopper and blend until smooth. Season with salt and pepper, then rub half of the oil over a 1¼ lb tuna loin. Leave to marinate for 10 minutes. Place a skillet over medium heat, then add the tuna and fry for 10–12 minutes, or until seared all over, turning frequently. Remove from the pan and slice thinly. Serve with a herby baby leaf salad sprinkled with toasted pine nuts, and the remaining basil oil.

Red Mullet with Capers and a Warm Tomato Salad

Serves 4

8 red mullet fillets, about 3½ oz each, scaled and gutted

finely grated zest of 1 lemon, plus 2 tablespoons juice

2 teaspoons baby capers, rinsed and drained

2 scallions, finely sliced

2½ cups mixed red and yellow cherry tomatoes

5 oz fine green beans, trimmed

2 garlic cloves, finely chopped

2 oz can anchovies, drained and chopped

1 tablespoon olive oil

2 tablespoons chopped parsley

salt and pepper

8 caperberries, to garnish

- Preheat the oven to 400°F. Tear off four large sheets of foil and line with parchment paper. Place 2 red mullet fillets on each piece of parchment, then scatter over the lemon zest, capers, and scallions. Season with salt and pepper. Fold the paper-lined foil over and pinch the edges together to seal. Place the parcels on a large cookie sheet.

- Put the cherry tomatoes in an ovenproof dish with the green beans, garlic, anchovies, oil, and lemon juice. Season with salt and pepper and mix well.

- Bake the vegetables in the oven for 10 minutes until tender. Place the fish next to the vegetables in the oven and bake for 8–10 minutes until the flesh flakes easily when pressed in the center with a knife.

- Remove the fish and vegetables from the oven. Spoon the vegetables onto warmed plates, then top with the steamed red mullet. Sprinkle over the chopped parsley, garnish with the caperberries, and serve immediately with slices of sourdough bread.

 Tomato Bruschetta with Anchovies

Heat a griddle pan and grill 4 slices of sourdough bread for 2–3 minutes until nicely charred on both sides. Halve 2½ cups red and yellow cherry tomatoes and toss with 8 capers, 2 finely sliced scallions, 2 tablespoons chopped parsley, and 1 tablespoon each of olive oil and aged sherry vinegar. Spoon the tomatoes over the bread. Top with 10 oz anchovy fillets and serve.

 Sun-Dried Tomato and Caper-Marinated Red Mullet Score several shallow slits into the skin of 8 scaled and gutted red mullet fillets, about 3½ oz each, and place them in an ovenproof dish. Mix together 2 tablespoons sun-dried tomato paste, 1 tablespoon caper paste (or 1 tablespoon rinsed capers, very finely chopped, if paste is unavailable), the finely grated zest of 1 lemon, 1 tablespoon olive oil, 1 finely chopped garlic clove, 2 tablespoons chopped parsley, and 1 oz can finely chopped drained anchovies. Rub the mixture over the red mullet fillets and set aside to marinate for about 10 minutes. Roast in a preheated oven at 400°F for about 10 minutes or until the flesh flakes easily when pressed in the center with a knife. Serve with steamed couscous and scattered with ½ cup anchovy-stuffed olives.

20 Aromatic Steamed Mussels

Serves 4

1 tablespoon peanut oil

2 shallots, thinly sliced

1 red chile, seeded and finely sliced

1 inch piece of fresh ginger root, peeled and finely chopped

1 garlic clove, finely sliced

3 tablespoons Pernod

1½ cups fish or vegetable stock

1 small preserved lemon, finely chopped

3 lb mussels, scrubbed and debearded

1 small bunch of cilantro, roughly chopped

salt and pepper

- Heat the oil in a large, heavy-based Dutch oven over medium-low heat, then stir in the shallots, chile, ginger root, and garlic. Cook gently for 7–8 minutes or until softened, stirring occasionally. Add the Pernod and simmer to evaporate. Then add the stock and preserved lemon and bring up to boiling point.

- Tip in the mussels, discarding any that won't close. Season with salt and pepper, then stir the mussels to coat them in the shallot mix. Cover the Dutch oven with a tight-fitting lid and steam gently, shaking the pan occasionally, for 4–5 minutes until the mussels are cooked. Part of the way through cooking, use a large metal spoon to stir the mussels thoroughly, lifting the ones from the bottom of the pan to the top. Replace the lid for the remaining cooking time until the mussels have opened, discarding any that remain closed.

- Heap the mussels into deep bowls, scatter over the cilantro, and serve immediately with a large bowl on the side for discarding the empty shells.

---

10 Thai Pan-Fried Mussels

Heat 1 tablespoon peanut oil in a skillet over medium heat, then add 2 thinly sliced shallots, ½ teaspoon minced chile from a jar, 1 teaspoon each finely chopped lemon grass and finely chopped ginger root, and ½ teaspoon finely chopped garlic. Cook gently for 3 minutes, then add 1¾ cups low-fat coconut milk. Simmer for 2 minutes, then stir in 13 oz cooked, shelled mussels and the cilantro. Bring to a boil and serve with rice.

30 Broiled Mussels Topped with Herbed Bread Crumbs

Cook 3 lb mussels, scrubbed and debearded as above. Remove one side from each mussel shell, discarding the empty half shells. Break in two any empty whole shells, discarding one half and sitting any loose mussels from the base of the pan inside the other half. Mix 1¼ cups coarse bread crumbs with the finely grated zest of 1 lemon and 1 large bunch of chopped cilantro. Arrange the shells on a large cookie sheet and scatter the bread crumbs over the mussels. Lightly spray the bread crumbs with light olive oil and slide under a preheated broiler for 2–3 minutes until crisp. Serve with a mixed salad.

30 Baked Salmon Fillets with Ginger and Chiles

Serves 4

1 inch piece of fresh ginger root, finely chopped

1 green chile, seeded and finely sliced

3 tablespoons chopped cilantro leaves

finely grated zest of 1 lime

1 teaspoon vegetable oil

1 tablespoon mirin

2 teaspoons fish sauce

4 chunky salmon fillets, about 4 oz each

13 oz mixed stir-fry vegetables

- Put the ginger root, chile, cilantro, lime zest, vegetable oil, mirin, and fish sauce into a mini chopper or small food processor bowl and blend to a paste.

- Place the salmon fillets in a shallow dish and rub all over with the paste. Set aside to marinate for 10 minutes.

- Preheat the oven to 400°F. Tear off four large sheets of foil and line with parchment paper. Put one-quarter of the stir-fry vegetables in the center of each piece of parchment, then top each heap with a salmon fillet. Bunch up the sides of the paper-lined foil to form an open parcel, then place on a cookie sheet. Bake in the oven for 10–12 minutes, or until the salmon is just cooked through.

- Remove from the oven and transfer the parcels to serving plates. Serve with steamed rice on the side, if liked.

---

1 **Thai Green Curry Salmon Stir-Fry** Cut 1¼ lb chunky salmon fillets into bite-size pieces. Heat 1 teaspoon vegetable oil in a large skillet over medium heat, then add 2 tablespoons low-fat coconut milk from a 13 oz can and 2–3 tablespoons green Thai curry paste. Stir-fry for 1 minute, then tip in the salmon and toss to coat. Add the remaining coconut milk, 2 teaspoons fish sauce, and 1 teaspoon palm sugar. Simmer gently for 3–4 minutes until the salmon is cooked. Serve with steamed rice and garnish with cilantro and lime wedges.

2 **Baked Salmon, Zucchini, and Asparagus with Feta** Slice 7 oz baby zucchini in half lengthways and toss with 8 oz trimmed asparagus and 1½ tablespoons olive oil. Season with salt and pepper, then place in a large roasting pan and put in a preheated oven at 400°F for 6–7 minutes. Meanwhile, take 4 chunky salmon fillets, about 4 oz each, wrap each in 1 slice of smoked salmon, and season with pepper. Remove the vegetables from the oven and place the salmon on top. Crumble over 3½ oz low-fat feta, scatter over 2 tablespoons pine nuts, and drizzle with 2 tablespoons lemon juice. Return to the oven and roast for 7–8 minutes, or until the salmon is just cooked. Serve with steamed Mediterranean couscous.

Skewered Teriyaki Cod with Steamed Ginger Rice

Serves 4

6 tablespoons teriyaki sauce
1 lb firm cod fillet, cut into
    bite-size pieces
1¾ cups Thai jasmine rice
1 teaspoon salt
2 tablespoons finely chopped
    fresh ginger root
8 scallions, trimmed
soy sauce, to serve

- Rub the teriyaki sauce over the pieces of cod and set aside to marinate.

- Put the rice in a saucepan with 3 cups of cold water, the salt, and the ginger root. Place the pan over medium-high heat, bring to a boil, and then reduce the heat to low and cover with a tight-fitting or foil-lined lid. Simmer gently for 12–14 minutes or until the water has been absorbed. Alternatively, cook in a rice cooker according to the manufacturer's instructions.

- Meanwhile, heat a ridged griddle pan and griddle the whole scallions for 3–4 minutes until tender and charred, turning occasionally.

- Thread the cod onto 4 metal skewers, then place on a foil-lined cookie sheet. Slide under a preheated broiler and broil for 2–3 minutes each side until cooked through.

- Serve the teriyaki cod with the rice, accompanied by the griddled scallions, and drizzled with any pan juices and a dash of soy sauce.

 Tuna Noodle Salad with Teriyaki Dressing Drain 2 x 6½ oz cans tuna chunks in brine or spring water and toss with a 10 oz bag of cooked, fresh rice noodles, 2 cups bean sprouts, and 1 seeded and thinly sliced red pepper. Divide among 4 serving plates. Mix 2 tablespoons teriyaki sauce with 1 tablespoon honey and 2 tablespoons each of light soy sauce and lime juice. Drizzle over the noodle salad and serve.

 Teriyaki Tuna Burgers To make a teriyaki glaze, in a small saucepan heat 4 tablespoons teriyaki sauce with 2 tablespoons honey, 2 tablespoons light soy sauce, 1 finely chopped garlic clove, 1 teaspoon peeled and finely grated fresh ginger root, and 1 teaspoon Japanese wasabi paste. When just starting to boil, lower the heat. Simmer to reduce the liquid by half. Meanwhile, finely chop 14½ oz raw tuna and mix with 1 finely chopped shallot and 1 teaspoon Japanese wasabi paste. Season with black pepper. Shape the tuna into 4 large burgers. Place 1 tablespoon vegetable oil in a large skillet over medium heat. Add the burgers and cook for 7–8 minutes until cooked through but still moist, turning and basting regularly with the teriyaki glaze. Meanwhile, griddle 8 trimmed scallions as above. Serve the burgers in toasted ciabatta-style rolls with 4 teaspoons mango chutney and the charred scallions.

30 North African Tuna Fattoush Salad

Serves 4

2 large eggs

2 large pita breads

2 tablespoons olive oil

4 tuna steaks, about 3½ oz each

4 Little Gem lettuces, sliced

2 scallions, sliced

1 small cucumber, seeded and chopped

3 tomatoes, quartered, seeded, and chopped

1 green pepper, cored, seeded, and chopped

3 tablespoons flat-leaf parsley, finely chopped

3 tablespoons mint, finely chopped

1–2 teaspoons harissa, to taste

2 tablespoons lemon juice

2 teaspoons crushed sumac, to sprinkle

salt and pepper

- Bring a small saucepan of water to a boil and add the eggs, being careful not to break the shells. Simmer gently for 6 minutes. Remove and cool under cold running water.

- Meanwhile, heat a ridged griddle pan and toast the pita breads for 2–3 minutes, turning once, until toasted and nicely charred.

- Rub 1 tablespoon of the olive oil over the tuna steaks, then season with salt and pepper. Place on a baking pan and slide under a preheated broiler for 3–4 minutes until almost cooked, turning once. Set aside to cool.

- Cut up the toasted pita bread and place in a large bowl with all the chopped vegetables and herbs. Mix together the harissa, lemon juice, and remaining olive oil. Stir into the salad to coat, then season generously with salt and pepper.

- Divide the salad onto serving plates. Cut the eggs into wedges and arrange over the salads. Top each salad with a tuna steak and serve sprinkled with the crushed sumac.

 Tuna Salad and Harissa Pitas

Warm 4 whole-wheat pita breads and split open. Spread the inside of each pita with ¼ teaspoon harissa and fill each one with 2 oz drained tuna in spring water, ½ sliced Little Gem lettuce, ¼ thinly sliced scallion, 4 thin slices of cucumber, 2 slices tomato, and 1 teaspoon each of chopped parsley and mint. Squeeze over 1 teaspoon lemon juice, season well, and serve.

 Grilled Tuna with Harissa-Spiced Pepper Sauce Add 1 tablespoon olive oil to a large, nonstick skillet over medium heat. Fry 2 sliced scallions and 1 seeded and chopped green pepper in the oil for 5–6 minutes until softened. Meanwhile, grill 4 tuna steaks, about 3½ oz each, as above. Add 4 roughly chopped tomatoes, 3 tablespoons chopped flat-leaf parsley, 3 tablespoons finely chopped mint, 1–2 teaspoons harissa, to taste, and 2 tablespoons lemon juice to the pan with the peppers. Stir to heat them through. Season generously with salt and pepper and spoon into serving bowls. Top each dish with a tuna steak and serve immediately with warmed pita breads.

30 Black Bean Chili with Monkfish on Toasted Tortilla

Serves 4

2 tablespoons peanut oil
1 teaspoon ground cumin
1 teaspoon ground coriander
¼ teaspoon ground cinnamon
¼ teaspoon dried red pepper flakes
13 oz monkfish tail, cubed
1 onion, finely chopped
2 garlic cloves, finely diced
¾ cup red wine
2 cups passata
13 oz can black beans, drained
few dashes of Tabasco sauce
4 large soft tortillas

Avocado salsa

1 large firm, ripe avocado
1½ tablespoons lime juice
½ small red onion, finely chopped
2 tomatoes, seeded and diced
1 small bunch of cilantro
salt and pepper

- Place the oil in a Dutch oven over medium heat. Add the spices and monkfish and cook for 2 minutes until lightly golden, stirring frequently. Remove the fish from the Dutch oven with a slotted spoon and set aside.

- Add the onion and garlic to the Dutch oven and cook for 5 minutes until softened, stirring frequently, then pour in the red wine and passata. Add the black beans and a few dashes of Tabasco, to taste. Season with salt and pepper and simmer for 12–15 minutes until thickened.

- To make the avocado salsa, remove the pit, then peel and dice the avocado. Gently mix it in a small bowl with the lime juice. Add the onion and tomatoes. Finely chop the cilantro and stir in, season, and mix well. Set aside.

- Stir the monkfish into the black bean chili and simmer for a further 2–3 minutes until the fish is just cooked.

- Meanwhile, set a ridged griddle pan over medium-hot heat, toast the tortillas, and place one on each plate. Spoon over the black bean chili and monkfish and serve immediately with the avocado salsa.

---

10 Black Bean and Monkfish Wrap

Toss 13 oz cubed monkfish tail with 1 teaspoon each of ground cumin and ground coriander, ¼ teaspoon each of ground cinnamon and dried red pepper flakes, and 2 finely chopped garlic cloves. Heat 1 tablespoon peanut oil in a nonstick pan over medium heat, add the coated monkfish, and fry, turning occasionally, for 5–6 minutes until just cooked through. Meanwhile, spread 5 oz low-fat guacamole over 4 soft tortillas and scatter over a 13 oz can of black beans, drained, ½ chopped small red onion, 1 chopped large bunch of cilantro, and 2 seeded and diced tomatoes. Divide the spiced monkfish onto the tortillas and roll up tightly. Cut in half and serve.

20 Monkfish and Black Bean Stir-Fry

Heat 1 tablespoon vegetable oil in a skillet, add 1 sliced onion and 2 sliced red peppers. Cook for 3 minutes, stirring. Add 2 finely chopped garlic cloves, 1 tablespoon finely chopped fresh ginger root, and stir. Add 13 oz cubed monkfish tail and cook for 3 minutes. Stir in a 13 oz can of black beans, drained, ¾ cup black bean stir-fry sauce, and 2 tablespoons soy sauce. Simmer for 2 minutes, then serve with rice.

 # Grilled Scallops with Chermoula Dressing

Serves 4

20 king scallops, without roes
11½ oz green beans, trimmed
5 oz mixed watercress and
spinach

Chermoula dressing

1 small bunch of flat-leaf parsley,
roughly chopped
1 small bunch of cilantro, roughly
chopped
½ teaspoon ground cumin
½ teaspoon ground coriander
½ teaspoon turmeric
½ teaspoon ras el hanout
1 garlic clove, finely chopped
4 tablespoons lemon juice
1 tablespoon olive oil
salt and pepper

- To make the chermoula dressing, put the herbs, spices, garlic, lemon juice, and oil in a mini chopper or a small food processor bowl. Blend until smooth, then season with salt and pepper.

- Place the scallops in a large bowl and pour over half of the chermoula dressing. Mix well to coat, then set aside to marinate for 8–10 minutes.

- Meanwhile, place the green beans in a basket steamer and lower into a shallow pan of boiling water so they are not quite touching the surface of the water. Steam for 3–4 minutes, or until just tender. Alternatively, cook in an electric steamer. Toss the cooked beans in half of the remaining dressing and set aside.

- Arrange the scallops on a baking pan and slide under a preheated broiler for 3–4 minutes until just cooked through, turning occasionally.

- Toss the beans with the watercress and spinach and divide onto serving plates. Top the salad with the broiled scallops. Serve immediately with the remaining dressing on the side.

 Pan-Fried Scallops with Chermoula Salad Season 20 king scallops, without roes, with salt and pepper and heat 1 tablespoon olive oil in a large skillet. Fry the scallops for 3–4 minutes, or until just cooked through, turning occasionally. Meanwhile, prepare the chermoula dressing as above. Halve 1¾ cups mixed cherry tomatoes and toss with 5 oz watercress. Divide between 4 serving plates. Arrange the scallops over the salads, drizzle with dressing, and serve.

 Grilled Scallops with Spiced Chickpea and Bean Salad Cook 11½ oz trimmed green beans as above. Heat 1 tablespoon olive oil in a skillet over medium heat, add 1 chopped onion and 2 chopped garlic cloves, and cook for 6–7 minutes, stirring occasionally. Stir in the chermoula spices as above and fry for a further minute. Pour in ¾ cup dry white wine, a 13 oz can drained chickpeas, and 1¾ cups halved cherry tomatoes. Simmer for 5–6 minutes, then stir in 1 small bunch of roughly chopped parsley, 1 small bunch of roughly chopped cilantro, and the finely grated zest and juice of 1 lemon. Season with salt and pepper to taste, then stir in the green beans. Meanwhile, rub 2 teaspoons olive oil over 20 king scallops without roes, season with salt and pepper, and slide under a preheated broiler for 3–4 minutes until just cooked through. Serve with the spiced chickpeas and beans.

30 Steamed Sea Bass with Lemon Grass, Ginger, and Noodles

Serves 4

2 scallions, trimmed
4 sea bass fillets, about 4 oz each
1 tablespoon peanut oil
1 garlic clove, finely sliced
¼ cup sake or Chinese cooking wine
11½ oz buckwheat soba noodles
2 teaspoons sesame seeds, to garnish

Marinade

2 teaspoons superfine sugar
2 tablespoons light soy sauce
2 lemon grass stalks, tough outer leaves removed
2 fresh lime leaves, shredded
1 inch piece of fresh ginger root, cut into thin matchsticks

- Slice the scallions very thinly lengthways and place in a bowl of cold water and ice cubes. Set aside in the fridge.

- To make the marinade, disolve the sugar in the soy sauce in a small bowl, then stir in the lemon grass, lime leaves, and ginger.

- Score small, shallow slits into the skin side of the fillets and place them in flat dish. Pour the marinade over and rub it into the flesh. Set aside to marinade for 15 minutes.

- Meanwhile, add the oil to a deep-sided skillet over medium heat. Fry the garlic for 2 minutes, then pour in the sake. Bubble to almost evaporate, then add the fish, skin-side down, and any marinade. Cover with a lid and steam for 6–8 minutes until the fish is just cooked and the flesh flakes easily.

- Cook the soba noodles in a large pan of boiling water for 7–8 minutes, or according to the package instructions, then drain.

- Remove the fillets from the pan, tip the noodles into the pan, and toss to coat in the cooking juices. Pile the noodles onto serving plates and place the sea bass on top. Drain the scallions and sprinkle over each fillet with the sesame seeds.

---

10 Sea Bass and Roast Vegetable Couscous

Heat 1 tablespoon olive oil in a large skillet over medium heat. Add 4 sea bass fillets, skin-side down, and fry for 3 minutes until golden. Reduce the heat, cover, and steam for 3–4 minutes, or until cooked. Divide 1 lb ready-made roasted vegetable couscous and 5 oz arugula among 4 plates. Mix 1 tablespoon vegetable oil with 1 teaspoon each of rice vinegar, finely chopped lemon grass, and ginger root. Drizzle over the salad and serve the fish on top.

20 Roasted Whole Sea Bass with Noodles and Sake Dressing

Score shallow slits into both sides of 4 small whole, gutted, and scaled sea bass. Mix 1 teaspoon finely grated fresh ginger root and 1 finely chopped garlic clove with 2 teaspoons sesame oil, then rub the mixture all over the inside and onto the skin of the sea bass. Place the fish in a nonstick roasting pan, sprinkle with 2 teaspoons sesame seeds, and place in a preheated oven at 400°F for 10–12 minutes until the flesh flakes easily when pressed in the center with a knife. Meanwhile, cook 11½ oz buckwheat soba noodles according to the package instructions. Place the marinade ingredients as above, and ¼ cup sake in a small saucepan. Place over medium-low heat and simmer for 4–5 minutes until fragrant. Serve the sea bass with the cooked noodles and drizzled with the hot aromatic sake.

20 Salt and Pepper Jumbo Shrimp with Baby Corn and Mango Salsa

Serves 4

1 teaspoon coarse sea salt

1 teaspoon Chinese 5-spice powder

1 teaspoon cracked black pepper

½ teaspoon Szechuan peppercorns, crushed

pinch of cayenne pepper

1 lb jumbo shrimp, shells on

8 low-fat soft flour tortillas

Baby corn and mango salsa

7 oz baby corn, sliced into small thin disks

2 scallions, trimmed and finely chopped

1 red chile, seeded and finely chopped

1 small mango, peeled, seeded, and diced

2 tablespoons sweet soy sauce (ketjap manis)

- Mix together in a large bowl the sea salt, Chinese 5-spice powder, and the black, Szechuan, and cayenne peppers. Then tip in the shrimp and toss until well coated.

- Heat a ridged griddled pan over high heat, arrange the shrimp on the pan, and cook for 4–5 minutes, or until the shrimp have turned pink and are cooked but still juicy.

- Meanwhile, to make the baby corn and mango salsa, mix together the baby corn, scallions, red chile, and diced mango. Then stir in the sweet soy sauce (ketjap manis).

- Once the shrimp are cooked, arrange them on serving plates with the tortillas and the mango salsa on the side (and a large bowl for discarding the shells).

10 Spicy Shrimp and Sweetcorn Salad

Toss 13 oz cooked, peeled shrimp with a 7 oz can of drained corn, 2 chopped scallions, 1 chopped red chile, and 1 diced mango. Combine 2 tablespoons each of sweet soy sauce and vegetable oil, then add black pepper, crushed Szechuan peppercorns, and pinch of cayenne pepper as above. Spoon the salad over the tortillas and serve drizzled with the dressing.

30 Peppered Shrimp, Baby Corn, and Mango Wraps

Mix 11½ oz raw, peeled shrimp with 1 teaspoon each of coarse sea salt, cracked black pepper, and Chinese 5-spice powder, ½ teaspoon crushed Szechuan peppercorns, and a pinch of cayenne pepper. Heat a ridged griddle pan over medium-high and cook the shrimp for 2–3 minutes as above. Remove from the heat and set aside to cool for 10–15 minutes.

Meanwhile, make the baby corn and mango salsa, as above. Soak 12 large rice paper wrappers in water for 2–3 minutes, or until soft, and thinly shred ½ an iceberg lettuce and 1 carrot. Take one wrapper and place a little lettuce and carrot in the center, then top with a few of the shrimp and a small spoonful of salsa. Fold in the sides and roll up firmly. Repeat with the remaining ingredients and serve immediately.

30 Stuffed Salmon with Ricotta and Spinach

Serves 4

1 lb new potatoes
4 salmon fillets, about 5 oz each
5 oz wild arugula
salt and pepper
lemon wedges, to serve

Ricotta and spinach filling

⅓ cup ricotta
1 teaspoon finely grated lemon zest
¼ teaspoon ground nutmeg
2 teaspoons wholegrain mustard
1 tablespoon chopped chives
3½ oz frozen spinach, defrosted, drained of excess water and roughly chopped

- Put the potatoes into a large saucepan and cover with lightly salted water. Bring to a boil and cook for 18–20 minutes until tender.

- Meanwhile, preheat the oven to 400°F and make the ricotta and spinach filling. Mix together the ricotta, lemon zest, nutmeg, wholegrain mustard, chives, and spinach. Season generously with salt and pepper.

- Place the salmon fillets on a nonstick baking pan and score a slit horizontally along the center of each fillet. Open out the slits and stuff each with the ricotta mixture. The mixture should fill the gap and create a little pile on top of each fillet.

- Bake the fillets in the oven for about 15 minutes, or until the flesh flakes easily when pressed in the center with a knife.

- Drain the new potatoes, then return them to the pan, crush with a fork, and season generously with salt and pepper. Serve the baked salmon with the crushed new potatoes, arugula, and lemon wedges.

---

10 Gravlax, Cream Cheese, and Spinach Open Sandwiches

Mix together ⅔ cup low-fat cream cheese, 1 teaspoon finely grated lemon zest, ¼ teaspoon ground nutmeg, 2 teaspoons wholegrain mustard, 1 tablespoon chopped chives, and 3½ oz frozen spinach, defrosted, drained, and roughly chopped. Season well with salt and pepper, then spread over 8 slices of rye bread. Top each with a thin slice of gravlax, season with black pepper, and serve with lemon wedges.

20 Smoked Salmon, Spinach, and Tomato Pasta

Bring a saucepan of lightly salted water to a boil and cook 13 oz farfalle pasta for 11 minutes until "al dente," or according to the package instructions. Drain and cool under cold running water. Meanwhile, place 4 oz baby leaf spinach in a large bowl with the finely grated zest and juice of 1 lemon, 1½ cups ready-to-eat, slow-roasted tomatoes (not in oil), and 7 oz smoked salmon, cut into strips. Tip in the cooked pasta and toss well. Divide the salmon pasta into serving bowls, drizzle over 1 tablespoon olive oil, and scatter over 1 tablespoon snipped chives and 2 tablespoons toasted mixed seeds. Serve immediately.

20 Smoked Mackerel Pasta Salad

Serves 4

10 oz conchiglie pasta

7 oz green beans, trimmed

4 hot-smoked peppered boneless mackerel fillets

4 oz mixed peppery salad

½ cucumber, cut in half lengthways, seeded, and cut into chunky pieces

2 scallions, finely sliced

2 hard-cooked eggs, quartered

Dressing

½ cup low-fat sour cream

1 tablespoon wholegrain mustard

1 teaspoon French mustard

2 tablespoons lemon juice

1 teaspoon chopped dill

1 teaspoon chopped tarragon

salt and pepper

- Bring a large saucepan of lightly salted water to a boil and cook the pasta for 11 minutes until "al dente," or according to the package instructions. Drain and cool under cold running water. Tip into a large bowl and set aside.

- Meanwhile, bring a medium-sized saucepan of lightly salted water to a boil and cook the beans in for 4–5 minutes until just tender. Drain into a colander, cool under cold running water, and set aside.

- To make the dressing, mix together in a small bowl all the ingredients and season with salt and pepper.

- Flake the smoked mackerel fillets into large pieces into the bowl with the cooled pasta, then add the salad leaves, cucumber, scallions, and cooked beans. Divide the pasta salad among serving bowls and top with the hard-cooked eggs. Serve with the dressing on the side.

10 Quick Smoked Mackerel Pâté

Put 4 hot-smoked peppered boneless mackerel fillets in a small food processor bowl or blender with 1 cup low-fat cream cheese with chives, 1 tablespoon horseradish sauce, 2 teaspoons lemon juice, and 1 teaspoon each of chopped dill and tarragon. Blend to a rough paste. Season with salt and pepper and serve with a selection of raw vegetable crudités or slices of hot toast.

30 Pan-Fried Mackerel with Grilled Polenta

Cut 1 lb ready-made polenta into ¾ inch slices and place under a preheated broiler for 5–6 minutes, turning once. Coat 4 fresh mackerel fillets, about 5 oz each, in 4 tablespoons flour and season with salt and pepper. Shake the fillets to remove any excess flour. Heat 1 tablespoon olive oil in a large, nonstick skillet over medium heat, then place the fillets skin-side down in the pan and cook, turning once, for 4–5 minutes, or until the flesh is opaque. Meanwhile, seed ½ a cucumber and use a mandolin or vegetable peeler to thinly slice it into long ribbons. Arrange the cucumber on serving plates with 4 oz peppery mixed salad greens and the polenta. Top with the crisp mackerel fillets and serve immediately with lemon wedges on the side.

LOW-FISH-BAE

30 Baked Haddock with Garlic Crumb Crust

Serves 4

2½ lb russet potatoes, peeled and chopped
1 tablespoon butter
2 leeks, trimmed and sliced
4 chunky, boneless haddock loins, about 5 oz each
light olive oil spray
2 tablespoons chopped chives
3 tablespoons half-fat crème fraîche
13 oz asparagus, steamed, to serve
lemon wedges, to serve
salt and pepper

Bread crumb topping

1¼ cups fresh bread crumbs
1 garlic clove, finely chopped
1 scallion, finely chopped
¼ cup pitted black olives, finely chopped

- Preheat the oven to 400°F. Boil the potatoes in a pan of salted water for 15 minutes until tender.

- Melt the butter in a small pan, add the leeks, and cover. Cook for 10–12 minutes, stirring, until softened and lightly golden. Place the haddock on a lightly greased baking pan.

- Meanwhile, make the bread crumb topping by mixing the bread crumbs with the garlic, scallions, olives, and 2–3 tablespoons water. Bring the mixture together and place clumps, slightly flattened, on top of the fish.

- Spray the fish lightly with oil spray and bake in the oven for 15–18 minutes until the bread crumbs are crisp and the flesh flakes easily when pressed in the center with a knife.

- Drain the potatoes and mash until smooth. Fold in the leeks, chives, and crème fraîche and season generously with salt and pepper. Spoon the mashed potatoes onto warmed serving plates and top with the haddock. Serve immediately with steamed asparagus and lemon wedges.

 Grilled Haddock with Toasted Bread Crumbs and Mashed Potatoes Place 4 thin haddock fillets, about 4 oz each, on a foil-lined baking pan, drizzle with 2 teaspoons olive oil, season with salt and pepper, and slide under a preheated broiler for 5–7 minutes, depending on the thickness of the fish, or until the flesh is white and flakes easily when pressed in the center with a knife. Meanwhile, make the bread crumb topping as above, replacing the water with 1 tablespoon light olive oil. Tip the topping into a large, nonstick skillet over medium heat and toast, stirring frequently, until crisp and golden. Heat 1¼ lb ready-made mashed potatoes and spoon onto serving plates. Place the haddock on top of the mashed potatoes and sprinkle over the toasted bread crumbs. Serve with lemon wedges on the side.

Smoked Haddock Potato Bake Warm 1 lb ready-made, low-fat cheese sauce in a large pan. Stir in 11½ oz skinless, cubed smoked haddock, 1¼ cups frozen peas, 5 oz can corn, drained, and 2 tablespoons snipped chives. Simmer for 3 minutes, then pour into an ovenproof dish. Cover with 1¼ lb ready-made mashed potatoes and sprinkle with 1 cup fresh bread crumbs. Bake in a preheated oven at 400°F for 10–12 minutes until crisp.

3 "Roast" Spiced Tuna Loin with New Potatoes and Asparagus

Serves 4

1 lb new potatoes
1½ lb tuna loin
1½ tablespoons olive oil
11½ oz trimmed asparagus tips
lemon wedges, to serve
  (optional)

Spice mix

2 teaspoons cumin seeds
2 teaspoons caraway seeds
2 teaspoons fennel seeds
1 teaspoon pink peppercorns

- Preheat the oven to 400°F. Put the potatoes into a large saucepan and cover with lightly salted water. Bring to a boil and cook for 15–18 minutes until tender. Drain and keep warm.

- Meanwhile, make the spice mix. Place all the spices in a spice grinder or mini chopper and grind to a coarse powder. Sprinkle the spices over a large plate.

- Rub the tuna loin with ½ tablespoon of the olive oil, then roll in the spice mix to coat. Heat the remaining oil in a skillet over medium heat, then sear the tuna for 8–10 minutes, turning frequently, until browned all over. Place the tuna in a small, nonstick roasting pan and bake in the oven for 10–12 minutes until cooked on the outside. Remove from the oven, cover with foil, and set aside to rest for 4–5 minutes.

- Heat a ridged griddle pan over high heat and cook the asparagus, turning occasionally, for 3–4 minutes until just tender and nicely charred. Once cooked, arrange on serving plates with the potatoes. Cut the tuna into slices and serve with the asparagus and lemon wedges, if liked.

---

1 Griddled Asparagus Tuna Niçoise

Cook 11½ oz trimmed asparagus tips in a basket steamer for 3–4 minutes until tender, then cool under cold running water. Pat dry with paper towels and arrange on serving plates with 6 oz arugula, 8 oz canned tuna fillets in spring water, drained, ½ thinly sliced red onion, and 2 sliced, hard-cooked eggs. Drizzle with 4 tablespoons low-fat herb dressing and serve immediately.

2 Spiced Griddled Tuna Loin with Potatoes and Asparagus

Cook 1 lb new potatoes in lightly salted boiling water and make the spice mix as above. Rub 1 tablespoon olive oil over 4 thick tuna steaks, about 5 oz each, and coat in the ground spice mix. Heat a ridged griddle pan over medium-high heat and griddle the tuna for 2–3 minutes each side, depending on the rareness desired. Remove from the heat and set aside to rest.

Meanwhile, steam 11½ oz trimmed asparagus tips in a basket steamer in a shallow pan of boiling water for 3–4 minutes until tender; make sure the basket is not quite touching the surface of the water. Arrange the asparagus and potato on serving plates, then top with the tuna steaks. Serve with lemon wedges on the side.

LOW-FISH-NOR

10 Lemony Scallop Skewers with Arugula

Serves 4

13 oz queen scallops, without roes
finely grated zest of 1 lemon, plus
  1 tablespoon juice
3 teaspoons basil oil
½ cup blanched hazelnuts
7 oz wild arugula
salt and pepper

- Preheat the broiler. Place the scallops in a bowl with the lemon zest and 2 teaspoons of the basil oil and season with black pepper. Mix well to coat, then thread the scallops onto 4 metal skewers.

- Slide the skewers under the broiler for 2–3 minutes, or until just cooked, turning occasionally. They are ready as soon as they are firm and opaque.

- Meanwhile, heat a small skillet over medium heat, then tip in the hazelnuts and dry-roast until golden, shaking the pan frequently. Tip the nuts into a small dish and crush lightly.

- Toss the arugula with the remaining basil oil, the lemon juice, and salt and pepper. Arrange on serving plates and top with the scallop skewers. Scatter over the hazelnuts and serve immediately.

 Scallops with Anchovies and Parma Ham Place 4 anchovy fillets in a mini chopper with 1 tablespoon capers, 1 teaspoon grated lemon zest, 2 tablespoons lemon juice, 1 small bunch of basil leaves, 1 small garlic clove, and 2 teaspoons basil oil. Blend until finely chopped, then season with salt and pepper. Heat 1 teaspoon basil oil in a nonstick pan. Add 4 slices thinly shredded Parma ham and fry until colored. Add 13 oz queen scallops, without roes, and plenty of black pepper. Fry for 2 minutes, or until the scallops are just cooked. Serve with arugula and the salsa verde.

 Grilled Scallops Wrapped In Parma Ham with Lemony Mashed Potatoes Cook 2 lb peeled potatoes in a large saucepan of lightly salted water for 18–20 minutes until tender. Drain and then mash with 2 tablespoons lemon juice and 2 teaspoons basil oil. Season with salt and pepper. Meanwhile, heat 1 tablespoon basil oil in a small skillet, add 2 chopped shallots, and cook until softened. Remove from the heat and mix with the finely grated zest of 1 lemon, some black pepper, 1¼ cups fresh bread crumbs, and ½ cup crushed dry-roasted blanched hazelnuts as above. Wrap 16 king scallops, without roes, in 16 lean strips of Parma ham and place in an ovenproof dish. Spoon the bread crumb topping onto the scallops, then slide under a preheated broiler for 7–8 minutes until the scallops are just cooked and the bread crumbs are golden. Serve with lemony mashed potatoes and arugula.

30 Salmon Wrapped in Ham with Pan-Roasted Potatoes and Beans

Serves 4

8 lean slices Black Forest ham
1 large bunch of basil, leaves stripped and shredded
4 chunky skinless salmon fillets, about 4 oz each, checked for pin bones
1 lb baby new potatoes
1 tablespoon olive oil
11½ oz scarlet runner beans, trimmed
8 oz green snap beans, trimmed
1 tablespoon lemon juice
salt and cracked black pepper
2 tablespoons balsamic glaze, to drizzle

- Lay the ham on a board to form 4 crosses. Scatter the center of each cross with a pinch of the shredded basil and some cracked black pepper. Place the salmon, skin-side up, on the basil and fold over the ham to completely enclose.

- Put the potatoes in a large saucepan with the olive oil and season with salt and pepper. Cover and fry gently over medium-low heat, shaking the pan frequently, for 20 minutes.

- Meanwhile, bring a saucepan of lightly salted water to a boil and cook the two types of beans for 2–3 minutes until firm but tender. Drain and toss with the lemon juice, remaining basil leaves, and some cracked black pepper.

- Heat a ridged griddle pan and cook the wrapped salmon fillets for 6–7 minutes, turning once, until the ham is golden and crisp and the salmon is almost cooked through. Remove from the heat and set the salmon aside to rest.

- Toss the cooked potatoes quickly with the dressed beans and spoon immediately onto warmed plates. Serve with the salmon parcels and drizzle with the balsamic glaze.

---

10 Smoked Salmon, Black Forest Ham and Basil Tagliatelle Cook 1 lb fresh tagliatelle in a large saucepan of salted boiling water, according to the package instructions. Drain and toss with 11½ oz flaked hot-smoked salmon, 2 tablespoons lemon juice, 1 large bunch of basil, leaves stripped and shredded, and 4 lean slices Black Forest ham, roughly chopped. Season with plenty of black pepper and serve with 6 oz peppery mixed salad greens.

20 Crispy Salmon Fillets with New Potatoes and Green Beans Chop 1 lb baby new potatoes in half and cook in a saucepan of lightly salted boiling water for 12–15 minutes until tender. Add 1 tablespoon olive oil to a large, nonstick skillet over medium heat. Fru 4 tail-end salmon fillets, about 4 oz each, skin-side down in the pan for 4–5 minutes until cooked but still moist. Once the skin is crisp, turn off the heat, scatter over the shredded basil leaves from 1 large bunch of basil, reserving a few whole leaves to garnish, and season with a little salt and pepper. Cover with a lid and set aside for 4–5 minutes to keep warm. Meanwhile, prepare and cook 11½ oz scarlet runner beans and 8 oz green snap beans as above. Transfer the potatoes and beans to serving plates and top with the salmon fillets. Garnish with the reserved whole basil leaves and serve with lemon wedges on the side.

Pasta with Tuna and Eggplant Arrabiata

Serves 4

1 tablespoon olive oil

1 onion, finely chopped

2 garlic cloves, finely chopped

1 eggplant, diced

1 lb 7 oz passata

½ cup red wine

½–1 teaspoon dried red pepper flakes, to taste

½ cup pitted green olives with hot chile peppers or chile-stuffed olives, sliced

leaves of 1 small bunch of basil

pinch of sugar

13 oz penne rigate

2 x 6½ oz cans tuna chunks in spring water, drained

finely grated Parmesan cheese, to serve (optional)

salt and pepper

- Place the oil in a large, deep-sided skillet over medium heat. Add the onion and garlic, and cook for 4–5 minutes, stirring occasionally, until softened and lightly golden.

- Bring two pans of lightly salted water to a boil. Add the eggplant to one saucepan and cook for 3–4 minutes until almost tender, then tip into a colander and drain well.

- Meanwhile, pour the passata and red wine into the pan with the onions, add the dried red pepper flakes, olives, basil, and sugar. Season with salt and pepper. Add the well-drained eggplant and bring to a boil, then reduce the heat and simmer gently for 12–15 minutes until thickened slightly.

- While the sauce is simmering, cook the pasta in the second pan of boiling water for 11 minutes until "al dente," or according to the package instructions.

- Drain the pasta. Stir the tuna into the sauce, add the pasta, and serve with a little Parmesan sprinkled over, if liked.

---

1 Pasta with Eggplant and Tomato Sauce

Cook 1 lb fresh penne in salted boiling water according to the package instructions. Meanwhile, roughly chop 6 ripe tomatoes and 7 oz grilled eggplant or mixed antipasti and fry over medium heat. Stir in ½ cup sliced chile-stuffed olives, chopped leaves from 1 small bunch of basil, and 1 seeded and finely chopped red chile. Drain the pasta, add the tomato mixture to the pasta, and toss to coat. Serve immediately.

3 Eggplant and Tomato Pasta Bake

Fry 1 finely chopped onion and 2 finely chopped garlic cloves in 1 tablespoon olive oil over medium heat until softened and lightly golden. Add ½ cup red wine, ½–1 teaspoon dried red pepper flakes flakes, to taste, ½ cup sliced pitted green olives with hot chile peppers or chile-stuffed olives, 7 oz well-drained, grilled eggplant or mixed antipasti, 2 x 13 oz can cherry tomatoes, and a pinch of sugar. Season well with salt and pepper, then simmer for 7–8 minutes until thickened slightly. Meanwhile, cook 1 lb fresh penne in lightly salted boiling water for 5–6 minutes until "al dente," or according to the package instructions. Drain the pasta and mix with the tomato sauce until well combined, then tip into an ovenproof dish, sprinkle with 2 tablespoons grated Parmesan cheese, and place in a preheated oven at 425°F for 12–15 minutes until bubbling and crispy. Serve with a crisp green salad.

LOW-FISH-PAD

QuickCook

Meat and Poultry

Recipes listed by cooking time

30

2

10

30 Grilled Tandoori Chicken Skewers with Cucumber and Cumin Salad

Serves 4

¾ cup fat-free Greek-style
 yogurt, plus extra to serve
2 tablespoons tandoori paste
1 lb skinless, boneless chicken
 breasts, cut into strips
2 teaspoons cumin seeds
1 small cucumber
½ red onion, cut in half and finely
 sliced
3 tablespoons fresh cilantro
 leaves
2 lemons, cut into wedges
salt and pepper
low-fat mini naan breads,
 to serve (optional)

- Mix together the yogurt and tandoori paste in a large bowl, add the chicken, and toss until the chicken is well coated. Set aside to marinate for 10 minutes.

- Heat a small skillet over medium heat, add the cumin seeds, and dry-roast for 1–2 minutes, stirring frequently. Remove from the heat when the seeds become fragrant and begin to smoke.

- Thread the chicken strips onto 4 metal skewers and lay on a foil-lined baking pan. Cook under a preheated broiler for 8–10 minutes until the chicken is cooked through, turning once.

- Meanwhile, slice the cucumber into ribbons using a sharp vegetable peeler and arrange on 4 serving plates. Scatter the onion and cilantro over the cucumber, sprinkle over the toasted cumin seeds, and season lightly with salt and pepper. Place the chicken and lemon wedges on top and serve immediately with warm naan breads and extra yogurt.

10 Tandoori Chicken and Salad Naans

Stir together 1 teaspoon tandoori paste and 6 tablespoons fat-free natural yogurt in a bowl. Roughly slice 10 oz cooked chicken fillets and mix with the tandoori yogurt. Cut ½ cucumber into ribbons, using a vegetable peeler, and finely slice ½ red onion. Divide the chicken among 4 low-fat mini naan breads, then divide the cucumber, onion, ½ teaspoon cumin seeds, and a few cilantro leaves into the naans. Squeeze a little lemon over the fillings and serve.

20 Grilled Tandoori Chicken

Cut 1 lb skinless chicken fillets into strips and mix with 2 tablespoons tandoori paste in a bowl to coat. Place the chicken on a foil-lined baking pan and slide under a preheated broiler for 6–7 minutes until cooked through, turning occasionally. Meanwhile, make a simple raita by mixing ¾ cup fat-free Greek-style yogurt, 2 teaspoons lemon juice, ¾ teaspoon ground cumin, and salt and pepper, to taste. Serve the chicken with the raita and warmed naan breads.

Asian-Spiced Beef Carpaccio

Serves 4

1 tablespoon peanut oil

1¼ lb fillet steak

2 cups bean sprouts

2 scallions, finely sliced

small bunch of mint, finely chopped

small bunch of cilantro, chopped

3 tablespoons chopped blanched peanuts (optional)

Dressing

1 tablespoon peanut oil

1 teaspoon fish sauce

2 teaspoons rice vinegar

2 tablespoons light soy sauce

2 teaspoons palm sugar

1 lemon grass stalk, outer leaves discarded, finely chopped

1 long shallot, finely chopped

1 red chile, seeded, finely sliced

- Heat the oil in a nonstick skillet over medium-hot heat, add the fillet steak, and sear for 4–5 minutes, turning frequently, until browned all over but still rare. Remove the fillet from the pan, pat dry with kitchen paper and cover in plastic wrap. Place in the freezer to chill for 20 minutes.

- Meanwhile, mix together all the dressing ingredients in a small bowl until well combined.

- In another bowl toss together the bean sprouts, scallion, and mint and cilantro leaves.

- Remove the beef from the freezer, discard the plastic wrap, and place on a cutting board. Slice the beef as thinly as possible, then arrange on 4 large plates, overlapping the slices slightly.

- Scatter the bean sprout mixture over the beef carpaccio, drizzle over the dressing, scatter with the peanuts. Serve immediately.

 Asian-Spiced Bean Sprout Salad with Roast Beef In a large bowl, mix together 1 tablespoon peanut oil, 1 teaspoon fish sauce, 2 teaspoons each of rice vinegar and palm sugar, 2 tablespoons light soy sauce, and 1 teaspoon each finely chopped lemon grass, finely grated fresh ginger root, and finely chopped red chile. Add 2 cups bean sprouts and toss to coat. Serve with 13 oz cooked and sliced rare beef, sprinkled with chopped cilantro and mint, and 3 tablespoons chopped peanuts.

Stir-Fried Beef Pancake Rolls Heat 1 tablespoon peanut oil in a wok over medium-high heat, add 1 sliced onion and stir-fry for 2 minutes. Add 1 tablespoon finely chopped fresh ginger root and 1 seeded and sliced medium red chile and stir-fry for a further 30 seconds. Add 10 oz thin beef strips and stir-fry for 2 minutes. Tip in 7 oz thinly sliced, mixed stir-fry vegetables and 2 cups bean sprouts. Cook for a further 2–3 minutes, then pour in 1 cup plum and hoisin stir-fry sauce and stir for 1 minute or until heated through. Serve with 12–16 Chinese pancakes, 2 trimmed and sliced scallions and ½ cucumber, cut into batons, to make pancake rolls at the table.

30 Piri-Piri Spiced Turkey Fillets and Hummus

Serves 4

14½ oz skinless, boneless turkey breasts, cut into strips
13 oz can chickpeas, drained
1 tablespoon lime juice
5–6 tablespoons low-fat sour cream
4 multiseed tortillas, warmed
lime wedges
salt and pepper

Piri-piri marinade

2 tablespoons sun-dried tomato puree
1 teaspoon oregano
2 tablespoons red wine vinegar
1 teaspoon hot smoked paprika
2 garlic cloves, finely chopped
2 long red chiles, finely chopped (remove seeds for less heat)

- To make the piri-piri marinade, put the tomato puree, oregano, red wine vinegar, paprika, garlic, and chiles in a mini chopper or a food processor. Season generously with salt and pepper, then blend until smooth.

- Tip the turkey strips into a bowl and scrape over the piri-piri marinade, reserving 1 tablespoon to make the hummus. Mix all the ingredients until the turkey is well coated, then set aside to marinate.

- Meanwhile, place the chickpeas, lime juice, and reserved piri-piri marinade in a food processor or blender and pulse briefly, adding enough sour cream to give a smooth, creamy consistency.

- Arrange the marinated turkey strips on a foil-lined baking pan and slide under a preheated broiler for 5–7 minutes, turning frequently, until cooked and lightly charred.

- Serve the grilled turkey fillets with the hummus, warmed tortillas, and lime wedges on the side.

 Griddled Tortilla with Piri-Piri Chicken Salad Heat a ridged griddle pan over medium-high heat and griddle the tortillas for 30–60 seconds each side, or until charred but still slightly soft. Push the tortillas into 4 small, deep serving bowls so that they line the bowls. Meanwhile, mix together 1 tablespoon ready-made piri-piri sauce and 6 tablespoons extra-light mayonnaise in a large bowl. Add 10 oz cooked, shredded turkey breast, then fold together until the turkey is well coated in the mayonnaise. Divide 1 shredded iceberg lettuce among the tortilla-lined bowls and then spoon the turkey mixture over the top of each. Sprinkle each salad with a pinch of hot smoked paprika and serve immediately with lime wedges on the side.

 Quick Piri-Piri Turkey Steaks with Hummus Enclose 4 turkey breast steaks in plastic wrap and flatten with a rolling pin. Unwrap and coat the turkey steaks with 4 tablespoons ready-made piri-piri sauce. Place on a foil-lined broiler pan and slide under a preheated broiler for 5–7 minutes until cooked, turning once. Stir 2 teaspoons of the ready-made piri-piri sauce into 1¼ cups low-fat hummus. Serve the turkey steaks with the hummus, warm tortillas, and lime wedges on the side.

LOW-MEAT-FOF

30 Beef and Baby Beet Salad with Horseradish Dressing

Serves 4

8 oz small, unpeeled baby beets, green stalks removed

2 lean rump or fillet steaks, about 7 oz each, trimmed

2 teaspoons olive oil

finely grated zest of 1 lemon and 1½ tablespoons lemon juice

1 garlic clove, finely chopped

2 tablespoons finely snipped chives

6 oz scarlet runner beans, sliced

1 teaspoon horseradish sauce

1 teaspoon honey

3 tablespoons low-fat sour cream

10 radishes, thinly sliced

½ cup walnut pieces

4 oz bistro-style salad greens

salt and pepper

- Cook the beets in a saucepan of boiling water for 10–25 minutes, depending on the size of the beets, until tender.

- Meanwhile, place the steaks in a shallow dish with the olive oil, lemon zest, garlic, 1 tablespoon of the snipped chives, and plenty of cracked black pepper. Toss until the steaks are well coated in the marinade.

- Bring another saucepan of water to a boil and cook the runner beans for 1–2 minutes until almost tender. Drain and cool immediately under cold running water.

- Heat a ridged griddle pan over medium-high heat and griddle the steaks for 1 minute each side until charred but still pink. Set aside in a warm place to rest.

- Mix the lemon juice, horseradish, honey, sour cream, and remaining chives in a bowl and season with salt and pepper. Drain the beets, cut into wedges, and toss with the cooked beans, radishes, walnuts, and salad greens, then heap onto serving plates. Slice the beef thinly and arrange over each salad, drizzle over the horseradish dressing, and serve.

---

10 Bistro-Style Salad with Rare Beef and Blue Cheese Dressing

Make the baby beet salad as above. Make a blue cheese dressing by combining 1½ tablespoons lemon juice, 1 teaspoon liquid honey, 1 tablespoon snipped chives, 3 tablespoons low-fat sour cream, and 2 oz strong blue cheese, such as Gorgonzola Piccante. Serve with 13 oz hand-carved, rare-cooked beef on top. Drizzle over the blue cheese dressing and serve.

20 Rare Beef and Blue Cheese Pasta

Cook 13 oz farfalle pasta in lightly salted boiling water for 11 minutes until "al dente," or according to the package instructions. Meanwhile, griddle 2 trimmed lean rump or fillet steaks, about 7 oz each, as above, and thinly slice. Make a blue cheese dressing by mixing together 1½ tablespoons lemon juice, 1 teaspoon honey, 1 tablespoon snipped chives, 3 tablespoons low-fat sour cream, and 2 oz strong blue cheese, such as Gorgonzola Piccante or Stilton, until well combined. Cook the runner beans in a saucepan of boiling water for 1–2 minutes until almost tender. Drain the pasta and mix with the blue cheese dressing, ½ cup walnuts pieces, the runner beans, and the beef. Garnish with snipped chives. Serve immediately with a bistro-style salad on the side.

LOW-MEAT-LYT

10 Chinese Chicken Wraps with Plum Sauce

Serves 4

4 large low-fat tortilla
  bread wraps
4 tablespoons plum sauce, plus
  extra to serve (optional)
10 oz cooked chicken breasts,
  such as sweet chile cooked
  chicken, sliced
½ cucumber, cut into batons
3 scallions, trimmed and finely
  sliced lengthways
1 large romaine lettuce heart,
  shredded

- Spread the tortilla bread wraps with the plum sauce, then top each wrap with the chicken, cucumber, and scallions. Finish with the romaine lettuce and roll up tightly.

- Cut in half diagonally and serve with a little extra plum sauce, if liked.

---

2 Steamed Chinese Chicken and Noodle Salad

Put 13 oz raw chicken strips, 1 teaspoon finely grated fresh ginger root, and 2 tablespoons dark soy sauce in a bowl and mix until the chicken is well coated. Place the chicken in a large basket steamer and lower into a shallow saucepan of boiling water so that the basket does not quite touch the surface of the water. Steam for 5–7 minutes until the chicken is cooked through. Set aside to cool. Meanwhile, cook 1 lb fresh noodles in boiling water for 2–3 minutes until tender, then drain into a colander and cool under cold running water. Toss together 1 shredded carrot, 1 thinly sliced red pepper, 2 cups bean sprouts, and the noodles in a large bowl. In a separate bowl mix together 4 tablespoons plum sauce, 1 teaspoon finely grated fresh ginger root, 1 teaspoon sesame oil, and 2 tablespoons light soy sauce. Scatter the steamed chicken over the noodles and drizzle with the dressing. Serve immediately.

3 Chicken Filo Pastries with Plum Sauce

Mix together in a bowl 13 oz cooked, shredded chicken, 3 finely sliced scallions, 1 grated carrot, 1 cup finely shredded sugar snap peas, and 1 finely chopped small bunch of cilantro until combined. Cut 8 sheets of filo pastry to 6 x 10 inches. Put one-eighth of the chicken mixture along the end of one rectangle, leaving a gap at the edge. Fold in the longer pastry sides, then roll up into a cigar shape. Brush with melted butter to seal. Repeat to make 8 pastries. Place on a lightly greased cookie sheet and cook in a preheated oven at 400°F for 18–20 minutes until golden and crisp. Serve with plum sauce.

30 Pork and Rosemary Meatballs with Mixed Bean Salad

Serves 4

1½ lb lean ground pork
1 cup fresh bread crumbs
1 egg, lightly beaten
1 tablespoon chopped rosemary
1 teaspoon fennel seeds, toasted
finely grated zest of 1 lemon
1 garlic clove, finely chopped
2 tablespoons olive oil
½ cup dry white wine
1 lb passata
salt and pepper

Warm bean salad

½ cup dry white wine
2 x 13 oz can lima beans
13 oz can cranberry beans
12 slow-roasted tomatoes (not in oil), chopped
1 teaspoon fennel seeds, toasted
juice of 1 lemon

- Place the ground pork, bread crumbs, egg, rosemary, fennel seeds, lemon zest, and garlic in a large bowl. Season with salt and pepper, then mix well to thoroughly combine. Shape into about 24 small meatballs.

- Heat the oil in a large, nonstick skillet over medium heat. Fry the meatballs, turning frequently, for 10–12 minutes, or until cooked through and browned all over.

- Pour ½ cup white wine into the pan with the meatballs and let bubble to evaporate. Add the passata and simmer for 10 minutes, occasionally scraping any sticky bits off of the bottom of the skillet.

- Meanwhile, to make the warm bean salad, pour the white wine into a large saucepan and bring to a boil. Drain the beans and add with the slow-roasted tomatoes and fennel seeds. Season with salt and pepper. Simmer for 5 minutes, then stir in 4 tablespoons of the sauce from the meatballs, the lemon juice, and the parsley. Spoon the bean mixture into serving bowls, top with the meatballs, and serve.

10 Warm Bean and Crisp Bacon Salad

Place 8 slices of lean smoked Canadian bacon under a preheated broiler and cook for 3–4 minutes until crisp, turning once. Meanwhile, pour ½ cup dry white wine into a large saucepan and bring to a boil. Add 2 drained 13 oz cans lima beans, 1 drained 13 oz can cranberry beans, 12 chopped ready-to-eat slow roasted tomatoes (not in oil), and 1 teaspoon toasted fennel seeds. Season with and salt and pepper and simmer for 5 minutes, then add the juice of 1 lemon and 1 chopped large bunch of parsley. Divide the warmed bean salad onto serving plates. Cut the bacon into slices and sprinkle over the beans. Serve with slices of warmed, herb bread.

20 Pork Skewers with Warm Bean Salad

Mix 1 tablespoon finely chopped rosemary, 2 teaspoons toasted fennel seeds, the zest of 1 lemon, and 1 tablespoon olive oil in a bowl. Tip in 1¼ lb lean pork loin, cubed, and toss until coated. Thread the pork onto 8 metal skewers and cook under a preheated broiler for 8–10 minutes, turning frequently. Make the bean salad as above, substituting the passata with 2 tablespoons sun-dried tomato puree. Serve with the warm salad.

LOW-MEAT-QYY

 # Turkey Burgers with Spicy Salsa

Serves 4

1 lb lean ground turkey
finely grated zest of 1 lime
3 scallions, trimmed
1 tablespoon sweet soy sauce
  (ketjap manis)
1 teaspoon ground cumin
1¼ cups fresh bread crumbs
1 small egg, lightly beaten
4 small ciabatta-style buns
2 romaine lettuce hearts,
  shredded, to serve

Spicy Salsa

1¾ cups cherry tomatoes,
  quartered
1 red chile, seeded and finely
  chopped
2 scallions, finely sliced
1 tablespoon lime juice
1 tablespoon sweet soy sauce
  (ketjap manis)
1 small bunch of cilantro, chopped
1 firm, ripe avocado

- Place the ground turkey in a large bowl with the lime zest, scallions, soy sauce, cumin, bread crumbs, and egg. Mix until well combined. Then form into 8 flattened patties.

- Transfer the burgers to a broiler pan and slide under a preheated broiler for 3–4 minutes each side, or until browned and cooked through.

- Meanwhile, make the spicy salsa by putting all the salsa ingredients in a bowl. Stir until well combined, then set aside.

- Cut the ciabatta rolls in half and place the rolls, cut-side up, on a broiler rack. Slide under a preheated broiler and toast for 1–2 minutes until lightly charred.

- When the burgers are ready, place them on the toasted rolls with the romaine lettuce leaves and top with the salsa. Serve as open-faced burgers.

 Healthy Turkey and Salsa Granary Baguettes Make the spicy salsa as above. Cut 4 small granary baguettes in half lengthways and fill each baguette with one-quarter of a 3 oz bag of mixed salad greens, 1 thick slice of cooked, hand-carved roast turkey, and 1–2 spoonfuls of the salsa. Serve immediately.

 Grilled Mini-Turkey Ball Skewers with Spicy Salsa Place 1 lb lean ground turkey, ½ finely chopped red onion, 1 finely chopped small bunch of parsley, 1 finely chopped red chile, and 1 teaspoon each of ground cumin, ground coriander, and fennel seeds in a bowl. Mix until well combined. Season well with salt and pepper and form into 32 small balls. Thread the balls onto 8 metal skewers. Place the skewers on a broiler pan and slide under a preheated broiler for 10–12 minutes until cooked through, turning occasionally. Meanwhile, make the spicy salsa as above. Serve the skewers with toasted ciabatta and the salsa.

30 Chili Con Carne

Serves 4

1 tablespoon peanut oil

1 large onion, chopped

1 lb lean beef, such as rump or
   fillet, cut into strips

2 garlic cloves, finely chopped

1 teaspoon ground cumin

1 teaspoon ground coriander

¼ teaspoon ground cinnamon

1–1½ teaspoons dried red pepper
   flakes, to taste

1 cup Mexican lager beer

1¼ lb thick passata

1 tablespoon Dijon mustard

13 oz can kidney beans, drained

long-grain rice, to serve

small bunch of cilantro, chopped,
   to garnish

- Heat the oil in a large, deep-sided skillet or a Dutch oven over medium heat. Fry the onions for 5–6 minutes, stirring occasionally, until lightly colored and just beginning to soften.

- Meanwhile, put the beef, garlic, ground spices, and dried red pepper flakes, to taste, in a bowl and toss until the beef is well coated. Scrape the beef into the pan with the onions, increase the heat to medium-high, and stir-fry for 1–2 minutes, or until the meat is browned.

- Add the lager beer, passata, mustard, and kidney beans to the pan and bring to a boil. Reduce the heat, then leave to cook at a quick simmer for about 20 minutes, or until thickened.

- Meanwhile, bring a large saucepan of lightly salted water to a boil and cook the rice for 15 minutes until tender, or according to the package instructions.

- Serve the chili with the rice or with baked potatoes, sprinkled with the cilantro and a dash of Tabasco, with lime wedges on the side, if liked.

 Quick Chili Con Carne Burgers

Combine 2 tablespoons chili con carne seasoning mix with 13 oz lean ground beef in a bowl. Form into 4 flattened burgers and set on a broiler pan under a preheated broiler for 2–3 minutes each side, or until cooked through. Serve with 4 whole-wheat buns and a handful of salad greens.

 Chili Con Carne and Lettuce Wraps

Cut 1 lb lean beef, such as rump or fillet, into strips. Put the beef in a bowl and mix with 2 finely chopped garlic cloves, 1 teaspoon each of ground cumin and coriander, ¼ teaspoon ground cinnamon, and 1–1½ teaspoons dried red pepper flakes, to taste, until combined. Heat 1 tablespoon peanut oil in a skillet, add the onion, and stir-fry for 4–5 minutes until soft. Add the beef and stir-fry for a further 4–5 minutes until cooked. Heap the beef and onion mixture onto 4 low-fat tortilla wraps. Top each wrap with ¼ of the drained beans from a 13 oz can, 1 shredded iceberg lettuce, a dollop of low-fat sour cream, and a few shakes of Tabasco sauce, and serve.

Sweet Chile Chicken Stir-Fry

Serves 4

1 tablespoon peanut oil

1 lb free-range chicken breast, cut into bite-size pieces

1 large onion, cut into large pieces

2 garlic cloves, sliced

1 tablespoon finely chopped fresh ginger root

3½ oz piece of pineapple, peeled and "eyes" remove, sliced, and cut into wedges

1 cup sweet chile stir-fry sauce

1 cup water chestnuts, halved

1 tablespoon soy sauce

1 tablespoon lime juice

1 cup frozen peas

2 tablespoons roughly chopped unsalted cashew nuts

- Heat the oil in a wok or large skillet over medium heat. Tip in the chicken pieces and cook for 3–4 minutes, stirring frequently, until golden brown all over. Remove from the heat with a slotted spoon and set aside.

- Add the onion to the wok and stir-fry for 2–3 minutes until golden and beginning to soften, then add the garlic and ginger root. Stir-fry for 1–2 minutes, then stir in the pineapple and sweet chile sauce. Bring to a boil.

- Return the chicken to the pan with the water chestnuts, soy sauce, and lime juice, and stir to combine. Reduce the heat and simmer gently for 4–6 minutes, or until the chicken is cooked through. Then add the peas and stir for 1–2 minutes until hot. Scatter over the cashew nuts and serve immediately with steamed rice.

 Quick Sweet Chile Chicken Stir-Fry

Heat 2 teaspoons peanut oil in a large skillet. Add 1 teaspoon each chopped garlic and ginger root. Stir-fry for 30 seconds. Add 13 oz prepared stir-fry vegetables and fry for 3–4 minutes, then add 13 oz cooked chicken slices, a 3½ oz piece of pineapple peeled and cut into bite-size wedges, 1 cup sweet chile stir-fry sauce, 1 tablespoon soy sauce, and 1 tablespoon lime juice. Stir until hot, then spoon into deep bowls over 2½ cups hot, cooked rice.

 Roasted Sweet Chile Chicken with Vegetable and Noodle Stir-Fry

Mix 1 lb lean mini chicken fillets with 6 tablespoons sweet chile sauce, 1 tablespoon soy sauce, and 1 teaspoon each of powdered onion and garlic. Place the chicken mixture on a nonstick baking pan and roast in a preheated oven at 400°F for 12–15 minutes until cooked through, turning once. Meanwhile, heat 2 teaspoons vegetable oil in a wok or skillet over medium heat. Add 13 oz stir-fry vegetables and cook for 2–3 minutes until beginning to wilt. Tip in 1 lb fresh noodles and stir-fry for 3 minutes, then toss through 2 tablespoons light soy sauce and 1 tablespoon lime juice. Serve the chicken fillets with the stir-fry vegetables and noodles with extra sweet chile dipping sauce on the side.

20 "Meat Feast" Thin and Crisp Pizza

Serves 4

10 oz thick passata
1 teaspoon lemon zest
pinch of sugar
1 teaspoon dried oregano
8 large, low-fat soft tortillas
3½ oz wafer-thin slices of lean smoked ham, roughly sliced
3½ oz wafer-thin slices lean turkey, roughly sliced
3 oz thinly sliced bresaola, roughly chopped
8 thin slices pepper-coated pastrami, roughly chopped
4 oz low-fat mozzarella cheese, cut into small dice
arugula, to serve

- Preheat the oven to 400°F. Put the passata, lemon zest, sugar, and oregano in a saucepan over medium-high heat. Season with salt and pepper, then bring almost to a boil. Reduce the heat and simmer gently for about 8 minutes or until thickened.

- Place 4 tortillas on a cookie sheet. Spoon ½ tablespoon of the sauce evenly over each tortilla. Place a second tortilla on top of the sauce to sandwich the tortillas together.

- Spread the remaining sauce evenly over four doubled-up bases and top with a selection of the different meats. Scatter over the mozzarella and cook in the oven for 8–10 minutes until crisp and bubbling. Serve scattered with arugula.

 Super-Quick "Meat Feast" Tortilla-Based Pizza Using 10 oz ready-made Italian tomato sauce and 8 large, low-fat soft tortillas, make up the pizza bases on a large cookie sheet as above. Sprinkle a 10 oz selection of thinly sliced and roughly chopped, lean continental cooked meats over the bases, then scatter over 1 cup grated low-fat cheddar cheese. Bake in a preheated oven at 400°F for 8–10 minutes until crisp and bubbling.

 "Meat Feast" Italian Pizza Make the sauce as above. Meanwhile, combine 1⅓ cups whole-wheat flour with 1 teaspoon each of fast-action yeast and superfine sugar, and ¾ teaspoon salt in a large bowl, making a well in the center. Pour in 1½ tablespoons olive oil and ½ cup hand-hot water, then knead the wet and dry ingredients together to make a smooth dough. Roll the dough out on a lightly floured surface so it is large enough to fit a large, nonstick cookie sheet, then place the rolled dough onto the cookie sheet. Using the tomato sauce and meat and mozzarella toppings as above, make up the pizza, then place in a preheated oven at 425°F for 12–15 minutes, or until crisp and bubbling.

30 Baked Chicken Parcels with Mozzarella and Basil

Serves 4

4 skinless, boneless chicken breasts, about 5 oz each

4 teaspoons red chile pesto or mild harissa

2 plum tomatoes, sliced

4 oz low-fat mozzarella, cut into 8 slices

1 small bunch of basil, leaves stripped

8 thin slices of lean chorizo

To serve

1 lb ready-made healthy couscous or bulghur salad

arugula

- Preheat the oven to 425°F. Place the chicken breasts between 2 large sheets of plastic wrap on a cutting board and beat with a rolling pin to flatten; they need to be about ¼ inch thick. Unwrap the chicken and spread 1 teaspoon of the pesto or mild harissa evenly over each flattened breast.

- Cover half of each chicken breast with 2–3 slices tomato and 2 slices mozzarella, then fold the uncovered half of the chicken over the filling to create a sandwich. Scatter the basil leaves over the top of the chicken parcels, reserving a few to garnish.

- Cover each parcel with 2 thin slices the chorizo, then secure with a wooden toothpick by threading it through the chicken breast. Arrange the parcels on a large, nonstick cookie sheet. Place in the oven for 15–18 minutes until cooked through.

- Serve the chicken parcels with the couscous or bulghur salad, and the arugula. Garnish with the reserved basil leaves.

 Chicken and Tomato Salad with Pesto Dressing Slice 13 oz cooked chicken fillets and arrange them on serving plates with 5 oz arugula, 2 tablespoons Parmesan cheese shavings, and 1¼ cups halved cherry tomatoes. Whisk 2 tablespoons pesto into 3 tablespoons aged balsamic vinegar and drizzle over the salad. Serve with warmed, sliced flatbreads.

 Grilled Chile Pesto Chicken with Warm Couscous Salad Flatten 4 skinless, boneless chicken breasts, about 5 oz each, as above, then spread 1 teaspoon chile pesto evenly over each one. Place the chicken on a large, foil-lined baking pan and slide under a preheated broiler for 7–8 minutes, or until cooked through, turning once. Squeeze over the juice of 1 lemon and rest for 2–3 minutes before slicing thickly.

Meanwhile, pour 1½ cups boiling water over 1¼ cups dried, roasted vegetable, or tomato couscous and stand for 5 minutes. Fluff up with a fork, then fold through 2 chopped plum tomatoes and 8 oz diced low-fat mozzarella. Spoon the couscous onto serving plates, then scatter over the torn leaves from 1 small bunch of basil and 12 pimiento-stuffed olives. Set the sliced grilled chicken on the top of the couscous, drizzle over any chicken juices, and serve.

30 Sweet and Spicy Pork with Red Peppers

Serves 4

1 tablespoon peanut oil

1 onion, thickly sliced

2 long sweet red peppers, seeded and diced

1 lb pork tenderloin, cubed

1 teaspoon fennel seeds

1 teaspoon finely grated lemon zest

1–2 tablespoons Thai chile paste (nam prik pao), to taste

¼ teaspoon dried red pepper flakes (optional)

2 teaspoons tamarind paste

2 tablespoons sweet soy sauce (ketjap manis)

13 oz can chopped tomatoes

3½ oz piece pineapple, peeled, "eyes" removed, diced, and lightly crushed

steamed rice, to serve

- Place the oil in a large, heavy-based skillet or flat-based wok over medium heat. Add the onion and peppers and cook for 7–8 minutes, or until softened, stirring occasionally.

- Add the pork and stir-fry for 1 minute to seal, then add the remaining ingredients. Simmer for 12–15 minutes until the pork is cooked and the sauce thickened. Serve with steamed rice.

---

1 Sweet and Sour Ground Pork and Pineapple Stir-Fry

Heat 1 tablespoon peanut oil in a large skillet over medium heat. Add 1 lb lean ground pork and stir-fry for 5–6 minutes until cooked. Stir in 1 cup sweet and sour sauce, a 3½ oz piece pineapple, peeled, diced, and lightly crushed, and 7 oz drained bamboo shoots. Simmer for 1–2 minutes until hot. Serve with steamed rice.

2 Sweet and Sour Chicken

Stir 2 tablespoons cornstarch into 1 tablespoon of water in a small bowl and set aside. Heat 1 tablespoon peanut oil in a large, nonstick skillet over medium heat. Add 3 roughly chopped scallions and 2 seeded and diced long red peppers to the pan. Stir-fry for 2–3 minutes. Tip in 13 oz cubed skinless, boneless chicken breast and stir-fry for 2–3 minutes to seal, then add a 3½ oz piece pineapple, peeled, "eyes" removed, diced, and lightly crushed, 2 roughly chopped tomatoes, the cornstarch mixture, 1 cup pineapple juice, 1 tablespoon rice vinegar, ¼ cup rice wine, and 2 tablespoons each of soy sauce and tomato ketchup. Bring to a boil and simmer gently for 8–10 minutes until the chicken is cooked and the sauce thickened. Serve with steamed rice.

20 Honey and Mustard Glazed Chicken Fillets with Coleslaw

Serves 4

3 tablespoons liquid honey

2 tablespoons wholegrain mustard

1 tablespoon Worcestershire sauce

1 tablespoon dark soy sauce

1¼ lb skinless, boneless mini
   chicken fillets

mixed salad greens, to serve

Coleslaw

½ red cabbage, shredded

½ small red onion, thinly sliced

1 large carrot, coarsely grated

4–6 tablespoons low-fat Caesar
   Salad dressing

- Preheat the oven to 400°F. Put the honey, mustard, Worcestershire sauce, and soy sauce in a large bowl and mix to combine. Tip in the chicken fillets and toss until the chicken is well coated in the glaze.

- Scrape the chicken into a foil-lined roasting pan, spreading it out over the base. Place in the oven for about 15 minutes, turning once, until cooked through.

- Meanwhile, to make the coleslaw, combine the cabbage, red onion, and carrot in a large bowl, then mix with 4–6 tablespoons of the Caesar Salad dressing, depending on the consistency desired.

- Serve the glazed fillets on top of a mixed salad greens together with the coleslaw on the side.

10 Honey and Mustard Chicken Slaw Salad

To make a honey and mustard dressing, combine 1 tablespoon honey, 1 tablespoon wholegrain mustard, 1½ tablespoons Worcestershire sauce, 2 teaspoons dark soy, and 2–3 tablespoons freshly squeezed orange juice in a jug or bowl. In a large bowl, toss together 13 oz cooked mini chicken fillets, ½ shredded red cabbage, ½ thinly sliced small red onion, and 1 coarsely grated large carrot. Arrange the chicken and cabbage salad on serving plates, scatter with 5 oz baked croutons, and drizzle over the dressing. Serve immediately.

30 Baked Jerk and Mustard Chicken and Coleslaw

Cut 3–4 deep slashes in 4 skinless, boneless free-range chicken breasts, about 5 oz each, and place on a foil-lined baking pan. Mix together 3 tablespoons honey, 2 tablespoons wholegrain mustard, 2 teaspoons jerk seasoning mix, and 1 finely chopped garlic clove. Massage the marinade into the chicken and put in a preheated oven at 400°F for 20–25 minutes until cooked through. Meanwhile, make the coleslaw as above. Serve the baked chicken breasts with the coleslaw and ½ a baked potato per person.

30 Chinese 5-Spice Duck with Ramen Noodles

Serves 4

1 teaspoon Chinese 5-spice powder

1 tablespoon liquid honey

2 tablespoons sweet soy sauce (ketjap manis)

2 large duck breasts, about 1 lb each, excess skin removed

4 cups clear chicken stock

1 garlic clove, thinly sliced

1 tablespoon finely chopped fresh ginger root

2 scallions, sliced diagonally

5 oz drained bamboo shoots

2 cups bean sprouts

11½ oz ramen noodles or medium egg noodles

2 teaspoons toasted sesame seeds, to serve

- Preheat the oven to 425°F. Put the Chinese 5-spice powder, honey, and 1 tablespoon of the sweet soy sauce (ketjap manis) in a bowl and mix. Take the duck breasts and score the skin with a sharp knife. Rub the 5-spice mixture into the scores and all over the skin and set aside for 5 minutes.

- Heat a skillet, add the duck breasts, skin-side down, and cook for 5–7 minutes, or until golden. Turn over and cook for a further 2–3 minutes. Transfer to a small roasting pan. Place in the oven for 5–10 minutes, or until cooked as desired.

- Meanwhile, put the stock, remaining sweet soy sauce, garlic, and ginger root in a saucepan over medium heat and bring to a gentle boil. Reduce the heat and simmer for 10 minutes, then add the scallions and bamboo shoots. Simmer for a further 2 minutes, then stir in the bean sprouts.

- In a separate saucepan cook the noodles in boiling water for 2–3 minutes, or according to the package instructions then drain. Remove the duck from the oven, leave to rest for 2–3 minutes, and slice thinly. Ladle the soup into deep bowls. Divide the noodles between the bowls, then arrange the sliced duck on top. Sprinkle with sesame seeds and serve.

10 Quick 5-Spice Noodle Soup

Put 4 cups vegetable stock, 1 teaspoon Chinese 5-spice paste, 2 tablespoons sweet soy sauce, and 1 teaspoon each of finely chopped garlic and fresh ginger root in a saucepan over medium-high heat. Bring to a gentle boil. Reduce the heat and simmer for 5–7 minutes. Meanwhile, diagonally slice 2 scallions and cut 7 oz firm tofu into slices. Reheat 14½ oz straight-to-wok medium noodles, according to the package instructions, and heap the noodles into deep bowls. Top the noodles with 2 cups bean sprouts and the tofu slices, then sprinkle with the scallions. Ladle over the hot soup and serve.

20 Duck and Egg Noodle Stir-Fry

Thinly slice 14½ oz duck fillets. Heat 2 teaspoons vegetable oil in a wok over medium heat, add 1 thinly sliced garlic clove, 1 tablespoon finely chopped fresh ginger root, and 2 sliced scallions, and stir-fry for 30 seconds. Add the duck and 1 lb fresh egg noodles. Stir-fry for 3 minutes, then stir in 1¼ cups Chinese-style stir-fry sauce and simmer for 1 minute before serving.

3⦿ Mild and Creamy Chicken Curry

Serves 4

1½ tablespoons peanut oil

1 large onion, sliced

2 garlic cloves, finely chopped

1 teaspoon ground turmeric

1 teaspoon ground cumin

1 teaspoon ground coriander

5 oz korma paste

1 lb skinless, boneless chicken breasts, cubed

8 oz sweet potato, peeled and cubed

¾ cup low-fat coconut milk

½ cup water

2 tablespoons ground almonds

1¼ cups basmati rice, washed

2 tablespoons chopped cilantro leaves, to garnish

low-fat naan bread, to serve (optional)

- Heat the oil in a saucepan or deep skillet over medium heat. Add the onion and cook for 5–6 minutes, or until softened, stirring frequently.

- Add the garlic, spices, and korma paste and stir-fry for 1–2 minutes, then stir in the chicken and sweet potato. Cook for 3–4 minutes to seal the chicken, then add the coconut milk, water, and ground almonds. Season with salt and pepper. Bring to a boil, then reduce the heat and simmer gently for 12–15 minutes, or until the chicken is cooked and the sweet potato cubes are tender.

- Meanwhile, put the basmati rice in a large pan of lightly salted boiling water and cook for 12 minutes until tender, or according to the package instructions.

- Serve the curry on a bed of rice, garnished with the cilantro. Offer some naan bread on the side, if liked.

1⦿ Cold Chicken Curry Salad with Rice

Mix together 1 cup fat-free Greek-style yogurt, ½ cup extra-light mayonnaise, 1 teaspoon curry powder, 3 tablespoons smooth mango chutney, 2 teaspoons lemon juice, and 2 tablespoons chopped cilantro in a large bowl. Roughly slice 13 oz tikka-roasted chicken mini fillets, then fold into the curry mayonnaise sauce. Serve with 2 cups cold, steamed wild basmati rice and lemon wedges.

2⦿ Grilled Korma Chicken with Rice

Cut 3–4 deep slashes in 4 skinless, boneless free-range chicken breasts, about 5 oz each, then cover each breast with 1 tablespoon korma paste. Place the chicken on a foil-lined baking pan and slide under a preheated broiler for 12–15 minutes, or until cooked, turning once. Serve with 2¾ cups cooked basmati rice, topped with a couple of dollops of fat-free plain yogurt, with lemon wedges on the side.

30 Lebanese-Spiced Lamb Skewers with Cucumber Salad

Serves 4

1 lb lean ground lamb
½ teaspoon ground nutmeg
½ teaspoon ground ginger
½ teaspoon ground allspice
½ teaspoon ground black pepper
½ teaspoon ground cinnamon
½ teaspoon ground cloves
1 garlic clove, finely chopped
2 tablespoons chopped mint
finely grated zest of 1 lemon
plus 1 tablespoon juice
salt and pepper
1–2 teaspoons sumac, (optional)

Cucumber salad

1 cucumber, seeded and finely
   chopped
1 green pepper, seeded and finely
   chopped
1 large bunch finely chopped parsley
1 large bunch finely chopped mint
3 tomatoes, seeded and chopped
juice of 1 lemon

- Put the ground lamb, ground spices, garlic, mint, lemon zest, and 1 tablespoon lemon juice in a large bowl. Season generously with salt and pepper, then mix all the ingredients together until well combined. Mold the spiced meat mixture into 8 slightly flattened sausage shapes. Then thread 2 sausages each onto 4 long metal skewers and set aside.

- Meanwhile, to make the cucumber salad, mix together the cucumber, pepper, parsley, mint, and tomatoes in a bowl. Season generously with salt and pepper, then stir in the remaining lemon juice. Set aside.

- Place the lamb skewers on a broiler rack, then slide under a preheated broiler for 6–7 minutes, turning once, until cooked through and browned all over.

- Arrange the salad onto serving plates, then place the lamb skewers on the salad. Sprinkle over the sumac, if using, and serve with griddled pita bread and lemon wedges, if liked.

 Baharat Spiced Lamb and Couscous

Mix 3 teaspoons baharat spice mix (or mix together the ground spices above) with 2 tablespoons each of lemon juice and chopped mint. Rub over 4 lean lamb steaks, about 4 oz each, and place under a preheated broiler for 4–6 minutes, or until cooked, turning once. Serve with quick-cook lemon and garlic couscous.

 Chawarma-Style Pita Lamb Kebabs

Mix together 3 teaspoons baharat spice mixture (or combine all the ground spices listed above) and 2 tablespoons each of lemon juice and chopped mint in a bowl. Rub the marinade over 4 lean lamb steaks, about 4 oz each, and place under a preheated broiler for 4–6 minutes, or until cooked to your liking, turning once. Meanwhile, make the cucumber salad as above. Slice the lamb thinly and stuff inside 4 large, warmed pitas. Spoon the cucumber salad into the pitas. Drizzle 3–4 tablespoons garlicky yogurt or tahini dressing over the salad. Serve sprinkled with 1–2 teaspoons sumac, if liked.

Chinese Pork and Vegetables

Serves 4

2 tablespoons liquid honey

2 tablespoons dark soy sauce

2 teaspoons Chinese 5-spice powder

1 teaspoon Szechuan pepper, lightly crushed

1 teaspoon finely grated fresh ginger root

2 teaspoons sesame oil

1 lb pork tenderloin, thickly sliced

1 red pepper, seeded and thinly sliced

1 lb Chinese cabbage, thinly sliced

2 cups bean sprouts

7 oz baby bok choy, cut in half lengthways

2 teaspoons sesame seeds, to serve

- Mix together the honey, soy sauce, Chinese 5-spice powder, Szechuan pepper, ginger root, and 1 teaspoon of the sesame oil in a bowl. Tip the pork into the bowl and massage the meat well with the marinade until coated.

- Heat a large, nonstick skillet over medium-high heat. Scrape the pork mixture into the pan and cook for 4–5 minutes, turning occasionally, until the pork is just cooked and tender.

- Meanwhile, heat the remaining 1 teaspoon sesame oil in a wok over medium-high heat, then add the red pepper, Chinese cabbage, bean sprouts, and baby bok choy. Stir-fry for 2–3 minutes until just tender.

- Remove the pork from the heat and serve immediately with the stir-fried vegetables and sprinkled with sesame seeds.

Ground Pork and Little Gem Stir-Fry

Heat 2 teaspoons sesame oil in a large skillet over medium heat. Add 1 lb lean ground pork. Fry for 5–6 minutes, or until cooked and browned. Stir in 2 tablespoons each of liquid honey and dark soy sauce, 2 teaspoons Chinese 5-spice power, and 1 teaspoon each of Szechuan peppercorns and grated fresh ginger root. Cook for a further 1–2 minutes, then serve with whole Little Gem lettuce leaves.

Chinese-Style Pan-Bake

Tip 1 seeded and thinly sliced red pepper, 1 lb thinly sliced Chinese cabbage, 2 cups bean sprouts, and 7 oz baby bok choy, cut in half lengthways, into a large nonstick roasting pan. In a large bowl mix together 2 tablespoons each liquid honey and dark soy sauce, 2 teaspoons Chinese 5-spice powder, 1 teaspoon Szechuan pepper, lightly crushed, 1 teaspoon finely grated fresh ginger root, and 2 teaspoons sesame oil. Add 1 lb thickly sliced pork tenderloin into the marinade and toss until the pork is well coated. Scatter the pork evenly over the vegetables in the roasting pan. Place in a preheated oven at 425°F for 18–20 minutes, or until just cooked and tender. Serve sprinkled with 2 teaspoons sesame seeds.

20 Baked Gnocchi with Smoked Turkey and Blue Cheese

Serves 4

1½ lb fresh gnocchi

½ cup extra-light cream cheese

4 oz strong blue cheese, such as Gorgonzola or Stilton

2 tablespoons snipped chives

7 oz cooked smoked turkey, cut into strips

7 oz frozen chopped spinach, defrosted

2 scallions, trimmed and thinly sliced

black pepper

- Preheat the oven to 425°F. Bring a large saucepan of lightly salted water to a boil and cook the gnocchi for 2 minutes until cooked through, or according to the package instructions. Drain well, then tip back into the saucepan.

- Meanwhile, gently warm the cream cheese, blue cheese, and chives in a skillet, then season with pepper. Remove from the heat, stir in the smoked turkey and spinach, and gently fold the sauce into the cooked gnocchi.

- Scrape the gnocchi and sauce into an ovenproof dish, scatter with the scallions, and place in the oven for 15–18 minutes until golden and bubbling.

- Serve the baked gnocchi with a crisp green salad and crusty bread, if liked.

10 Baby Gnocchi with Creamy Blue Cheese and Turkey Sauce

Cook 1½ lb tricolor baby gnocchi as above. Drain and spoon into deep bowls. Meanwhile, melt 4 oz Gorgonzola with 1 cup low-fat light cream in a pan over low heat, stirring continuously. Add 2 tablespoons snipped chives and season with black pepper. Simmer for 1–2 minutes, take off the heat, and stir in 7 oz cooked smoked turkey, cut into strips. Pour the sauce over the gnocchi and serve with sliced scallions.

30 Gnocchi, Squash, Sweet Potato, and Blue Cheese Bake

Chop 10 oz each butternut squash and sweet potato and add to a saucepan of lightly salted boiling water. Cook for 15 minutes, or until tender. Drain into a colander, then tip back into the saucepan and crush slightly with a fork. Meanwhile, make the smoked turkey and blue cheese sauce as above. Then cook 1 lb potato gnocchi or tricolor baby gnocchi in a large saucepan of lightly salted boiling water for 2 minutes, or according to the package instructions. Mix the gnocchi through the sauce, then fold through the crushed butternut squash and sweet potato. Scrape all the ingredients into an ovenproof dish, sprinkle over 2 trimmed and sliced scallions. Bake in a preheated oven at 450°F for 12 minutes until bubbling. Serve with a green salad.

10 Fast-Seared Steak with Green Snap Beans

Serves 4

13 oz green snap beans, trimmed
1 teaspoon olive ol
4 thin frying steaks
7 oz arugula
salt and pepper
crusty baguette, to serve

Tomato dressing

2 tomatoes, diced
1 teaspoon olive oil
1 long shallot, finely chopped
1 tablespoon wholegrain mustard
1 tablespoon red wine vinegar

- Bring a saucepan of lightly salted water to the boil, then add the green beans and cook for 2–3 minutes until tender but firm.

- Meanwhile, to make the tomato dressing, put the tomatoes, oil, shallot, mustard, and red wine vinegar in a bowl and mix to combine.

- Drain the beans and return to the pan. Toss the tomato dressing through the beans, season generously with salt and pepper, cover, and keep warm.

- Heat a large ridged griddle pan over high heat. Rub the oil over the steaks, then cook the steaks in the griddle pan for 1 minute each side. Remove and rest for 1–2 minutes.

- Divide the arugula onto serving plates. Spoon the beans and their dressing over the arugula, then top each plate with a seared steak. Serve immediately with crusty French baguette.

---

2 Peppered Steak with Wilted Spinach, Capers, and Tomatoes Heat 2 teaspoons olive oil in small skillet over medium heat. Add 1 finely sliced long shallot and 2 finely chopped garlic cloves and cook for 5–6 minutes until softened, stirring occasionally. Add 4 seeded and chopped tomatoes, 1½ tablespoons rinsed capers, and 1 tablespoon red wine vinegar. Cook gently for 2–3 minutes to heat through, then stir in 7 oz baby spinach until just wilted. Meanwhile, rub 1 teaspoon olive oil over 4 lean rump steaks, about 5 oz each. Coat the steaks generously in coarsely ground black pepper and place on a hot griddle pan over medium-high heat. Cook the steaks for 2–3 minutes each side. Meanwhile cook 13 oz trimmed green snap beans in boiling water for 2–3 minutes until tender. Serve the beans with the warmed tomato and spinach and peppered steak.

3 Pan-Fried Steak with New Potatoes and Arugula Cook 1 lb halved baby new potatoes in 2 cups vegetable stock, or enough stock to just cover the potatoes. Cover the pan with foil and a lid and simmer for 15–18 minutes until tender. Meanwhile, make the tomato dressing, as above. Rub 4 fillet steaks, about 5 oz each, with 1 teaspoon olive oil and season with salt and pepper. Cook as above for 2–4 minutes each side. Serve with the potatoes and 7 oz arugula tossed with the tomato dressing.

30 Crisp Garlic Baked Stuffed Chicken Breasts

Serves 4

4 free-range skinless, boneless
   chicken breasts, about 5 oz each
⅓ cup low-fat cream cheese
1 large garlic clove, finely chopped
2 tablespoons chopped parsley
½ tablespoon lemon juice
1 teaspoon finely grated lemon
   zest
½ cup all-purpose flour
1 large egg, beaten
¾ cup dried white bread crumbs
salt and pepper

To serve

1 lb new potatoes
3 cups broccoli florets

- Preheat the oven to 425°F. Cut deep slits along the sides of the chicken breasts to create a pocket in each. Mix together the cream cheese, garlic, parsley, and lemon juice and zest. Season well with salt and pepper, then spoon the filling into the slits in the chicken.

- Place the flour, egg, and bread crumbs in separate shallow dishes. Coat each chicken breast first in the flour, then the egg, and then the bread crumbs. Arrange on a baking pan and place in the oven for 15–18 minutes, or until cooked.

- Meanwhile, cook the new potatoes in a saucepan of lightly salted boiling water for 15–18 minutes until tender.

- Cook the broccoli florets in a large basket steamer for 3–4 minutes until tender. Alternatively, cook in an electric steamer, according to the manufacturer's instructions.

- Serve the crisp baked chicken with the broccoli and new potatoes.

 Garlicky Cream Cheese and Chicken Rolls Cut 4 ciabatta-style rolls in half and toast, cut-side down, on a ridged griddle pan over medium heat until golden and nicely charred. Rub the toasted sides of the rolls with the cut sides of 1 garlic clove, then spread the bases with ⅓ cup low-fat cream cheese. Scatter over 3 oz baby leaf salad greens, then top with 10 oz cooked chicken slices. Squeeze over a little lemon juice and top the bases with the other half of the rolls.

 Chicken Fillets in Garlic and Herb Bread crumbs Mix together ¾ cup dried white bread crumbs with 1 teaspoon each of garlic powder and dried herbes de Provence in a shallow dish. Put ½ cup all-purpose flour in a separate dish and 1 beaten egg in another dish. Coat 1 lb skinless, boneless mini chicken fillets in the flour, then the egg, then in bread crumbs, and arrange on a baking pan. Place in a preheated oven at 425°F for 12–15 minutes until cooked, then serve with mashed potatoes and a salad.

 # Moroccan Grilled Lamb with Golden Raisins

Serves 4

2 cups lamb stock
¾ cup golden raisins
1 large preserved lemon, chopped
4 lean lamb fillets, about 5 oz each
2 cups couscous
1 teaspoon olive oil
1–2 tablespoons toasted flaked almonds, to garnish

Spicy yogurt paste

2 garlic cloves, finely chopped
2 tablespoons finely chopped mint
1 teaspoon ground coriander
1 teaspoon ground cumin
¼ teaspoon ground ginger
1 tablespoon lemon juice
6 tablespoons fat-free plain yogurt
½ teaspoon harissa

- Pour the lamb stock into a saucepan over low heat, add the golden raisins and preserved lemon, and heat to almost simmering. Remove from the heat, cover, and keep warm.

- Make the spicy yogurt paste by mixing together all the ingredients in a small bowl. Add more harissa, if liked.

- Slice the lamb fillets in half lengthways, without quite cutting all the way through. Open up the fillets like a butterfly and massage the spicy yogurt paste into the meat.

- Place the couscous, olive oil, and a pinch of salt in a bowl and mix until all the grains are coated in the oil. Stir in the hot lamb stock with the golden raisins and preserved lemon, then cover and set aside in a warm place for 12–15 minutes, or until the couscous is tender and the liquid is absorbed.

- Meanwhile, cook the lamb fillets under a preheated broiler for 6–8 minutes, turning once, or until cooked as desired. Leave to rest covered loosely with foil. Heap the couscous onto serving plates and top with the lamb. Scatter over the toasted almonds and serve.

 ### Moroccan-Spiced Lamb with Couscous

Make the spicy yogurt paste as above, then rub over 4 lean lamb steaks, about 4 oz each. Broil the lamb for 2–3 minutes each side or as desired. Meanwhile, put ½ cup raisins in a small pan, cover with boiling water, and simmer for 3–4 minutes to swell. Serve the lamb with 1 lb low-fat, ready-made roasted vegetable couscous salad, and top with the drained raisins and 1–2 tablespoons toasted flaked almonds.

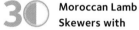 ### Moroccan Lamb Skewers with Preserved Lemon Couscous

Make the spicy yogurt paste in a large bowl as above. Cut 1 lb lean lamb leg meat into cubes, tip into the paste, and mix until coated. Set aside to marinate for 10 minutes. Meanwhile, place 2 cups couscous in a large bowl with 1 teaspoon olive oil and a pinch of salt and mix until the grains are coated in the oil. Stir in 2 cups hot lamb stock, ¾ cup golden raisins, and 1 chopped large preserved lemon. Cover and set aside in a warm place for 12–15 minutes until all the liquid has been absorbed. Cut 2 zucchini and 1 red onion into chunks and thread onto 4 metal skewers with the lamb. Place the skewers under a preheated broiler for 7–8 minutes or until cooked as desired, turning frequently. Serve the skewers with the couscous. Scatter over toasted flaked almonds, if liked.

20 Quick Beef Bolognaise

Serves 4

1 onion, roughly chopped
1 carrot, roughly chopped
1 celery stick, trimmed and
  roughly chopped
1 large field mushroom, about
  3½ oz, roughly chopped
1 tablespoon olive oil
2 garlic cloves, finely chopped
11½ oz lean ground beef
13 oz spaghetti
10 oz low-fat, Italian-style fresh
  tomato sauce for pasta
1¼ cups boiling water
½ teaspoon finely grated lemon
  zest
½ teaspoon dried oregano
4 teaspoons grated Parmesan
  cheese, to serve (optional)
salt and pepper

- Put the onion, carrots, celery, and mushroom in a food processor or blender and pulse until finely chopped.

- Heat the olive oil in a large, deep-sided skillet over medium heat, tip in the chopped vegetables, and cook for 3 minutes, stirring occasionally. Add the garlic and cook for 2–3 minutes, or until softened, stirring frequently. Tip in the ground beef, increase the heat to high, and cook for 2–3 minutes until browned.

- Meanwhile, bring a large saucepan of lightly salted water to the boil and cook the spaghetti for 11 minutes until "al dente," or according to the package instructions.

- Pour the tomato sauce for pasta into the pan with the meat. Add the measured boiling water, lemon zest, and oregano. Season with salt and pepper, reduce the heat, cover loosely, and simmer for about 10 minutes, or until thickened.

- Drain the pasta and serve in deep bowls topped with the bolognaise sauce and a little grated Parmesan, if liked.

---

10 Ground Beef and Tomato Spaghetti

Heat 1 tablespoon olive oil in a large, nonstick skillet over medium heat and add 1 lb lean ground beef. Fry for 5–6 minutes until browned and cooked. Add 1¼ lb fresh tomato-based pasta sauce to the meat and stir to heat through. Serve with 1 lb cooked fresh spaghetti.

30 Penne Bolognaise Bake

Cook 10 oz penne in lightly salted boiling water for about 10 minutes until "al dente," or according to the package instructions. Make the quick beef bolognaise as above, then stir into the drained pasta. Scrape into an ovenproof dish, sprinkle over 2 tablespoons grated Parmesan cheese, and place in a preheated oven at 450°F for 8–10 minutes, or until bubbling.

3⏺ Roast Pork Tenderloin with Lemon, Sage, and Capers

Serves 4

2 thin pork tenderloins, about
 10 oz each, cut in half
1 garlic clove, roughly chopped
1 tablespoon chopped sage leaves
finely grated zest and juice of
 1 lemon
4 teaspoons olive oil
2 teaspoons liquid honey
1 tablespoon capers, rinsed and
 drained
2 long shallots, chopped
10 oz baby leaf spinach, roughly
 sliced
8–12 caperberries, to garnish
salt and pepper

- Preheat the oven to 425°F. Slice the pork tenderloin lengthways without quite cutting all the way through and open up like a butterfly.

- Place the garlic, sage, lemon zest, 2 teaspoons olive oil, honey, capers, and 1 teaspoon of lemon juice in a mini chopper and blend to a rough paste. Rub the mixture all over the pork.

- Heat a skillet over medium heat, add the pork, and fry for 1 minute to seal, turning once. Transfer the pork to a small roasting pan, season with salt and pepper, and roast in the oven for 10 minutes or until cooked and the juices run clear. Remove from the oven, cover with foil, and set aside to rest.

- Meanwhile, heat the remaining oil in a skillet over low heat, add the shallots, and cook for 5–6 minutes, or until softened. Add the spinach and stir until wilted. Stir in the remaining lemon juice, season with salt and pepper, then spoon onto serving plates. Place the pork on top and scatter over caperberries to serve.

1⏺ Pan-Fried Pork with Lemon, Sage, and Honey Dressing

Cut in half 2 thin pork tenderloins, about 10 oz each, and place between 2 sheets of plastic wrap. Flatten the tenderloins with a rolling pin, uncover, and season with salt and pepper. Heat 2 teaspoons olive oil in a skillet over medium heat, add the tenderloins, and fry for 1–2 minutes each side until browned and cooked through. Cover the tenderloins with foil and set aside to rest.

Meanwhile, make a dressing by combining 2 tablespoons olive oil, the juice of 1 lemon, 1 tablespoon chopped sage leaves, and 1 teaspoon liquid honey. Mix any juices from the cooked tenderloins into the dressing, then pour the dressing over the pork slices. Serve with 6 oz baby spinach.

2⏺ Pork Medallions with Lemon and Caper Sauce

Slice 2 thin pork tenderloins, about 10 oz each, into ¾ inch medallions. Heat 4 teaspoons olive oil in a skillet and cook the pork for 1–2 minutes on each side. Add 1 chopped garlic clove, finely grated zest of 1 lemon, 1 tablespoon each of chopped sage leaves and capers, 2 teaspoons liquid honey, and ¾ cup dry white wine. Simmer for 2–3 minutes until the pork is cooked. Serve with wilted spinach as above.

20 Serrano Ham and Watercress Salad with Avocado

Serves 4

1 long granary or multigrain
baguette, cut into large cubes

1 tablespoon avocado oil, plus
extra to serve (optional)

4 oz watercress

8 thin Serrano ham slices

4 plum tomatoes, sliced

2 ripe but firm Hass avocados,
peeled, pitted, and sliced

3–4 teaspoons raspberry vinegar,
plus extra to serve (optional)

½ cup walnut pieces (optional)

salt and pepper

- Preheat the oven to 350°F. Scatter the baguette cubes over a large baking sheet, drizzle with avocado oil, and season with salt. Cook the cubes in the oven for 10–12 minutes until crisp and golden. Remove from the oven and set aside to cool.

- Put the watercress onto serving plates and arrange the slices of ham, tomato, and avocado over them. Scatter over the cooled croutons, then drizzle with raspberry vinegar, to taste, and season generously with pepper.

- Scatter with the walnuts, if using, and serve drizzled with a little extra avocado oil and raspberry vinegar, if liked.

10 Avocado, Serrano Ham, and Watercress Sandwiches

Crush together 2 ripe avocados, 1 teaspoon raspberry vinegar, and ½ cup walnut pieces in a bowl. Season with salt and pepper. Slice open 4 small crusty granary baguettes, then spread the avocado mixture over the bases and scatter with 4 oz watercress. Layer 2 thin slices Serrano ham over each baguette. Serve as open-faced sandwiches, drizzled with avocado oil and seasoned with cracked black pepper.

30 Warmed Roasted Tomato and Serrano Ham Pasta

Place 2 cups mixed red and yellow cherry tomatoes in a nonstick roasting pan. Sprinkle with 2 finely sliced garlic cloves and 2 tablespoons olive oil. Season generously with salt and pepper. Roast the tomatoes in a preheated oven at 350°F for about 25 minutes or until cooked and beginning to burst. Meanwhile, cook 11½ oz tricolor pasta in lightly salted boiling water for 11 minutes until "al dente," or according to the package instructions. Drain the pasta into a colander and cool under cold running water. Then tip the pasta into a bowl and toss with 3–4 tablespoons raspberry vinegar, to taste, 8 thin slices of Serrano ham, cut into strips, and ½ cup walnut pieces. Add the roasted tomatoes to the bowl and toss gently through the pasta. Serve warm with a watercress and avocado salad on the side.

LOW-MEAT-DOV

30 Stuffed Pork Steaks with Lima Bean Salad

Serves 4

4 thick lean pork loin steaks, about 7 oz each
1½ tablespoons olive oil
2 garlic cloves, finely chopped
finely grated zest of 1 lemon
1 teaspoon fennel seeds
4 oz light mozzarella
½ cup dry white wine
salt and pepper

Lima bean salad

1½ tablespoons olive oil
1 red onion, finely sliced
2 teaspoons fennel seeds
13 oz can lima beans
½ cup pitted kalamata olives, roughly chopped
10 oz sweet baby plum tomatoes, cut into quarters
8 slow-roasted, ready-to-eat tomatoes (not in oil), chopped
1 small bunch of basil, chopped
6 oz roasted red peppers
2 tablespoons lemon juice

- Preheat the oven to 425°F. Cut slits along the sides of the pork loin steaks to create a pocket in each. Mix together the olive oil, garlic, lemon zest, fennel seeds, and pepper, to taste, in a small bowl. Rub the mixture all over the steaks, including inside the pockets. Slice the mozzarella into 8 and stuff 2 slices inside each pocket.

- Heat a large, nonstick skillet over medium-high heat, add the pork steaks, and fry for 1–2 minutes each side until golden. Pour the white wine over the steaks and bring up to a boil. Remove the pan from the heat and transfer the pork to a snug-fitting ovenproof dish. Pour over the wine and juices and put in the oven for about 15 minutes, or until just cooked through and tender.

- Meanwhile, to make the bean salad, heat the olive oil in a clean skillet over medium-low heat, add the onion and fennel seeds, and cook for 7–8 minutes until softened, stirring occasionally. Drain the beans and add with the olives, tomatoes, basil, and roasted peppers to the pan, season with salt and pepper, and heat until the salad is warm. Stir through the lemon juice, then spoon onto serving plates.

- Top each plate of bean salad with a pork steak, drizzle over any juices remaining in the pan, and serve immediately.

---

10 Bean Salad with Mozzarella and Parma Ham

In a bowl, mix a 13 oz can lima beans, drained, with 10 oz sweet baby plum tomatoes, cut into quarters, ½ cup roughly chopped pitted kalamata olives, 8 chopped slow-roasted, ready-to-eat tomatoes (not in oil), 2 teaspoons fennel seeds, ½ teaspoon olive oil, and 2 tablespoons lemon juice until well combined. Spoon the bean salad onto serving plates, then tear 4 oz light mozzarella cheese into pieces and scatter over the salads. Toss 4 oz arugula and 2 thin slices lean Parma ham through each plate of bean salad and mozzarella and serve.

20 Grilled Pork with Bean Salad

In a small bowl mix 2 teaspoons fennel seeds, the grated zest of 1 lemon, 2 finely chopped garlic cloves, and pepper to taste. Rub over 4 lean pork steaks. Broil for 6–8 minutes, or until golden and cooked through, turning once. Serve with bean salad as above.

30 Chicken Risotto with White Wine and Asparagus

Serves 4

1½ tablespoons canola oil

1 small onion, finely chopped

8 oz lean, boneless, skinless
chicken thighs, diced

1¾ cups risotto rice

¾ cup dry white wine

4 cups hot chicken stock

8.oz asparagus stalks, trimmed

2 tablespoons low-fat
mascarpone cheese

pepper

- Add the oil to a large, deep-sided skillet over medium-high heat. Fry the onion in the oil for 4–5 minutes, or until softened, stirring occasionally. Add the chicken and stir-fry for 2 minutes until browned.

- Stir in the rice, then pour in the dry white wine. Simmer rapidly, stirring constantly, until the liquid has been absorbed.

- Reduce the heat, add a small ladleful of the hot chicken stock, and stir constantly at a gentle simmer until the stock has been absorbed. Repeat this process until all the stock has been absorbed and the rice is "al dente"—about 17 minutes.

- Stir the mascarpone into the rice, cover the pan with a lid, and set aside to rest for 2–3 minutes.

- Meanwhile, place the asparagus stalks in a basket steamer and cook for 2–3 minutes until tender.

- Spoon the risotto onto serving plates, season with pepper, and serve with the asparagus.

 Creamy Rice with Chicken and Mushrooms Fry 2½ cups chopped crimini mushrooms in 1½ tablespoons canola oil over medium-high heat for 3–4 minutes, then pour in ½ cup vermouth and 10 oz roughly chopped, cooked chicken. Simmer rapidly to evaporate the vermouth, then stir in 1 cup hot chicken stock, 2 tablespoons low-fat mascarpone, and 2¼ cups cooked long-grain rice. Season with salt and pepper and serve.

Chicken, Mushroom, and Asparagus Risotto Pour 3¾ cups chicken or vegetable stock into a saucepan and heat to a gentle boil. Fry 1 finely chopped small onion in 1½ tablespoons canola oil in a skillet over medium-high heat for 3–4 minutes, then add 8 oz diced lean, boneless, skinless chicken thighs. Stir-fry to brown the meat, then pour in ¾ cup dry white wine. Simmer rapidly to burn off the alcohol, then stir in 2 x 6 oz packages of quick-cook mushroom risotto. Add the boiling stock and simmer gently for 12 minutes until "al dente," stirring occasionally. Meanwhile, place 8 oz trimmed asparagus stalks in a basket steamer and lower into a shallow pan of simmering water so that the basket does not quite touch the surface of the water. Cook for 2–3 minutes until tender. Stir 2 tablespoons low-fat mascarpone into the risotto, if liked, then serve the risotto in deep bowls topped with the asparagus.

30 Poached Poussin with Baby Vegetables

Serves 4

2 poussin, about 14½ oz each, cut in half lengthways

7 oz baby zucchini, cut in half lengthways

7 oz baby carrots, cut in half lengthways

5 oz baby leeks, cut in half lengthways

4–6 cups good-quality chicken stock

1 bouquet garni made with fresh parsley, bay leaves, and thyme

4 oz fine asparagus tips, trimmed

1 baby green cabbage, cut into thin wedges

salt and pepper

- Place the poussin in a large Dutch oven with the baby vegetables, asparagus, and cabbage. Pour in enough chicken stock to almost cover the poussins. Add the bouquet garni, then place over high heat and bring to a boil. Reduce the heat and simmer gently for 15–18 minutes, or until the poussins are cooked and the vegetables are tender. Season with salt and pepper.

- Remove the bouquet garni from the Dutch oven and peel and discard the skins off of the poussin. Serve the poussin in deep dishes with the vegetables and plenty of broth.

 Lemony Chargrilled Asparagus and Chicken Salad Toss 1 lb trimmed asparagus spears in 1 tablespoon olive oil. Heat a ridged griddle pan over high heat and griddle the asparagus for 4–5 minutes until tender and charred, turning frequently. Meanwhile, roughly slice 13 oz poached or roasted chicken breast and toss with 8 oz mixed baby leaf salad greens. Arrange the chicken and greens on serving plates and top with the asparagus. Drizzle over 4 tablespoons low-fat, lemony salad dressing and serve.

 Thai Red Curry Chicken and Vegetable Broth Cut 7 oz baby zucchini and 7 oz baby carrots into thin batons, slice 4 oz trimmed fine asparagus tips lengthways, and thinly shred 1 baby green cabbage. Heat 2 teaspoons vegetable oil in a wok over medium heat, then add the vegetables and stir-fry for 3–4 minutes until beginning to soften. Add 2 tablespoons Thai red curry paste and stir-fry for 1 minute, then add a 13 oz can low-fat coconut milk, 1¾ cups hot chicken stock, 2 tablespoons fish sauce, and 10 oz sliced chicken breast. Simmer gently for 4–5 minutes, or until the chicken is cooked. Meanwhile, heat 12 oz cooked rice noodles. Spoon the noodles into serving bowls, ladle over the broth, and serve.

3⦾ Madeira and Rosemary Pork Medallions

Serves 4

½ cup dry-packed sun-dried tomatoes

2½ lb large potatoes, peeled and quartered

2 tablespoons olive oil

1½ lb pork fillet, cut into ¾ inch slices

3 shallots, finely sliced

¼ cup Madeira

4 teaspoons finely chopped rosemary

½ cup low-fat light cream

1 tablespoon wholegrain mustard

⅓ cup low-fat milk

salt and pepper

- Place the sun-dried tomatoes in a bowl and cover with just-boiled water. Cover the bowl and set aside for 20 minutes.

- Put the potatoes in a large saucepan and cover with salted water. Bring to a boil and cook for 15–20 minutes.

- Heat the olive oil in a large skillet over medium-high heat, add the pork, and cook for 1–2 minutes until golden, turning once. Remove from the pan and set aside.

- Reduce the heat to medium, add the shallots to the pan, and cook for 4–5 minutes until softened and golden. Pour in the Madeira and add 2 teaspoons of the rosemary. Allow to bubble, then stir in the cream, season generously with salt and pepper, and simmer for 1–2 minutes to heat through.

- Drain the soaked tomatoes, reserving 2 tablespoons of the soaking liquid, then slice into strips. Add the pork, tomatoes, and reserved liquid to the pan. Simmer gently for 3–4 minutes.

- Meanwhile, drain the potatoes and mash with the mustard, remaining rosemary, and milk. Season well with salt and pepper and serve with the pork medallions placed on top.

1⦾ Smoked Bacon and Rosemary Pasta

Sauce Cut 4 slices of lean, smoked Canadian bacon into strips and fry in 1 tablespoon olive oil until crisp. Add 3 finely chopped shallots, stir-fry for 2–3 minutes, then add ½ cup thinly sliced sun-dried tomatoes in oil, drained, 4 teaspoons finely chopped rosemary, and ¼ cup Madeira. Let it bubble up, add ½ cup low-fat light cream, season, and simmer until hot. Serve with cooked fresh tagliatelle.

2⦾ Pan-Fried Pork Loin with Rosemary and Cider Vinegar

Sauce Heat 2 teaspoons olive oil in a large skillet over medium heat, then add 4 lean pork loin steaks, about 5 oz each, and fry for 1–2 minutes each side, or until browned. Remove the steaks from the pan and set aside. Add 2 chopped slices of lean smoked bacon to the pan. Stir-fry for 2–3 minutes, then add 3 finely chopped shallots and cook for 3–4 minutes, stirring occasionally.

Add 4 teaspoons finely chopped rosemary, ½ cup dry cider, and ¼ cup cider vinegar and return the pork to the pan. Simmer gently for 3–4 minutes until the pork is cooked through, then stir in ½ cup low-fat light cream and heat until the sauce is hot. Serve with steamed purple sprouting broccoli.

Turkey Breast with Prosciutto, Sage, and Capers

Serves 4

4 turkey breast fillet steaks or scallops, about 5 oz each

8 lean slices prosciutto or Parma ham

8 sage leaves

2 tablespoons all-purpose flour

light olive oil spray

1 lb fresh tagliatelle

2 tablespoons Marsala

½ cup dry white wine

1 tablespoon capers, rinsed and drained, or 8 caperberries

pepper

- Place a turkey scallop between 2 layers of plastic wrap. Flatten with a rolling pin. Discard the wrap, then fold a slice of ham in half and place it over the turkey. Top with 2 sage leaves and secure with toothpicks. Repeat with the other escalopes. Season the flour with pepper and sprinkle on top.

- Place a large, nonstick skillet over medium-high heat, spray with a little oil, and fry the turkey in batches for 2–3 minutes on each side until golden brown.

- Meanwhile, bring a large saucepan of salted water to the boil and cook the tagliatelle for 3–4 minutes until "al dente," or according to the package instructions, then drain.

- Add the Marsala to the pan with the escalopes, followed by the white wine and capers, scraping the base gently with a wooden spatula to deglaze the pan. Turn the escalopes over and let the sauce bubble gently for another 1–2 minutes

- Transfer the pasta to serving plates, place the escalopes on top, and spoon over the juices to serve.

Chicken, Prosciutto, and Sage Open Ciabatta Sandwich

Split open 4 ciabatta rolls and griddle the cut sides on a ridged griddle pan over medium-high heat. Top each ciabatta base with 2 oz thickly sliced cooked chicken, a slice of prosciutto or Parma ham, 2 slices of beefsteak tomato, 1 finely chopped sage leaf, and ½ teaspoon rinsed and drained capers. Season with black pepper, top with a small handful of lamb's lettuce, and serve as an open sandwich with the lid resting by the base.

Roasted Turkey, Prosciutto, Sage, and Caperberry Rolls

Prepare the turkey scallops as above, layering them with the ham and sage leaves but without securing with toothpicks. Roughly chop 8 caperberries and scatter over the scallops. Roll up each piece of turkey tightly, now securing each with a toothpick. Arrange the rolls in a shallow, ovenproof dish and place in a preheated oven at 400°F for 10 minutes. Add 2 tablespoons marsala and ½ cup dry white wine to the dish, then bake for a further 8–10 minutes until the turkey is cooked through. Remove and serve, cut in half diagonally, with 1 lb cooked fresh tagliatelle.

30 Grilled Pork Skewers with Crunchy Coleslaw

Serves 4

1 lb 3½ oz lean pork loin, cubed
1 tablespoon red wine vinegar
2 teaspoons piri-piri sauce
½ teaspoon granulated sugar
4–6 tablespoons extra-light
   mayonnaise
½ red cabbage, shredded
2 carrots, grated
2 scallions, trimmed and thinly
   sliced
salt and pepper

Barbecue marinade

2 tablespoons Barbados sugar
2 tablespoons tomato ketchup
2 tablespoons dark soy sauce
1 teaspoon Chinese 5-spice powder
2 tablespoons freshly squeezed
   orange juice

- To make the barbecue marinade, combine the Barbados sugar, tomato ketchup, soy sauce, Chinese 5-spice powder, and orange juice in a large bowl until smooth. Tip the pork loin cubes into the bowl and mix until the pork is well coated with the marinade. Set aside to marinate for 15 minutes.

- Combine the vinegar, piri-piri sauce, granulated sugar, and mayonnaise in a small bowl to make the coleslaw dressing. Toss the cabbage, carrots, and scallions together in a large bowl, then add the dressing and mix until all the ingredients are well coated. Season with salt and pepper and set aside.

- Preheat the broiler. Thread the marinated pork onto 8 metal skewers, set them on the broiler pan, and slide under the broiler for 7–10 minutes, turning occasionally, until cooked through and sticky.

- Serve the pork skewers with the coleslaw and with sticky Thai rice, if liked.

---

10 Spicy Broiled Pork Steaks Smother 6 thin, lean pork loin steaks, about 14½ oz total weight, with 6 tablespoons ready-made spicy barbecue marinade. Place on a broiler pan. Broil for 7–8 minutes until cooked and sticky, turning once and brushing with extra marinade. When the pork is cooked, carefully cut into strips and serve with 14½ oz ready-made, low-fat coleslaw. Sprinkle with a few dashes of piri-piri sauce to season and serve immediately.

20 Braised Pork in an Orange Barbecue Sauce Make the barbecue marinade as above, adding an extra ⅓ cup freshly squeezed orange juice. Pour the marinade into a large saucepan over low heat and warm gently to dissolve the sugar. Add 1 lb 2 oz cubed lean pork loin and simmer gently for 10–12 minutes until just cooked through. Serve with steamed sticky Thai rice, steamed sugar snap peas, and scatter with 2 sliced scallions.

QuickCook

Vegetarian

Recipes listed by cooking time

3⊗

2

10

30 Quinoa-Stuffed Beefsteak Tomatoes with Melting Mozzarella

Serves 4

1¾ cups vegetable stock

1 cup quinoa, rinsed under running water

1 tablespoon canola oil

2½ cups crimini mushrooms, chopped

2 small zucchini, diced

2 scallions, finely chopped

2 tablespoons toasted sunflower seeds

1 small bunch of chopped basil

finely grated zest of 1 lemon

8 small or 4 large tomatoes

4 oz low-fat mozzarella, sliced

salt and pepper

- Pour the vegetable stock into a medium-sized saucepan and bring to a boil. Tip the quinoa into the pan, cover, and simmer gently for 12–15 minutes. It is ready when the seed begins to come away from the germ. Remove from the heat and drain off any stock that hasn't been absorbed.

- Meanwhile, preheat the oven to 400°F and heat the oil in a large skillet over medium heat. Add the mushrooms and cook, stirring, for 4–5 minutes. Then add the zucchini and cook for a further 4–5 minutes. Stir in the scallions, sunflower seeds, basil, lemon zest, and cooked quinoa. Season well with salt and pepper.

- Cut the tops off the tomatoes and scoop out the seeds. Spoon the quinoa mixture into the tomatoes, then top each tomato with the sliced mozzarella. Place on a greased baking pan. Replace the lids, then bake in the oven for 15–18 minutes, or until the mozzarella melts. Serve with a crisp green salad.

10 Mixed Vegetable Quinoa

Cook the quinoa as above. Meanwhile, heat 1 tablespoon canola oil in a large skillet over medium heat. Add 2½ cups chopped crimini mushrooms and stir-fry for 4–5 minutes, then add 1¾ cups defrosted frozen peas, 7 oz can corn, drained, 2 chopped scallions, and 1 chopped small bunch of basil. Stir-fry until heated through, then remove from the heat, toss through the quinoa, and scatter over 4 oz diced mozzarella. Serve with lemon wedges and a green salad.

20 Grilled Mushroom and Couscous-Stuffed Tomatoes

Heat 1 tablespoon canola oil in a large skillet over medium heat, then add 2½ cups chopped crimini mushrooms and fry for 4–5 minutes, stirring occasionally. Meanwhile, pour 1½ cups boiling water over 1¼ cups quick-cook roasted vegetable couscous and leave to stand for 5 minutes. Fluff the couscous with a fork, then mix through the cooked mushrooms, 2 tablespoons each of chopped parsley and mint, the grated zest of 1 lemon, and 1 cored, seeded, and finely chopped green pepper. Cut the tops off 8 small or 4 large tomatoes, then stuff with the couscous mixture. Crumble 5 oz low-fat feta over the tops, place the tomatoes on a broiler pan, and slide under a preheated broiler for 5–6 minutes until hot and golden. Serve with lemon wedges and salad greens.

20 Chile-Spiked Broccoli with Linguine

Serves 4

13 oz linguine

1½ tablespoons olive oil

2 garlic cloves, finely sliced

1 large red chile, finely chopped

3 tablespoons lemon juice

¾ cup vegetable stock

10 oz broccoli rabe, cut into 1–1½ inch pieces, or broccoli florets

2–3 tablespoons pecorino cheese with black pepper or mature pecorino, finely grated (optional)

salt and pepper

- Bring a large pan of lightly salted water to a boil and cook the linguine for 11 minutes until "al dente," or according to the package instructions.

- Meanwhile, heat the olive oil in a small skillet over low heat. Add the garlic and chile and cook gently for 3–4 minutes until tender. Stir in the lemon juice and vegetable stock and bring to a boil.

- Add the broccoli rabe or florets to the stock, then cover and simmer gently for 2–3 minutes until just "al dente," turning occasionally. Season generously with salt and pepper.

- Toss the broccoli and chile-spiked stock gently with the drained pasta, then heap into deep bowls. Serve immediately, sprinkled with the grated pecorino, if using.

10 Chile-Spiked Asparagus with Penne

Cook 1 lb fresh penne in salted boiling water for 4–5 minutes until "al dente," or according to the package instructions. Meanwhile, heat 1½ tablespoons olive oil in a small skillet over low heat. Add 2 finely sliced garlic cloves and 1 finely chopped large red chile and cook gently for 3–4 minutes. Stir in 3 tablespoons lemon juice and ½ cup vegetable stock and bring to a boil. Tip in 10 oz trimmed asparagus tips, cover, and simmer gently for 2–3 minutes until "al dente," turning occasionally. Season generously with salt and pepper, then toss with the penne.

30 Creamy Chile-Spiked Baked Penne

Cook 1 lb fresh penne in lightly salted boiling water for 4–5 minutes until "al dente," or according to the package instructions, adding 10 oz broccoli florets for the final 3 minutes of cooking. Meanwhile, heat 1½ tablespoons olive oil in a small skillet over low heat, then add 2 finely sliced garlic cloves and 1 large finely chopped red chile. Cook gently for 3–4 minutes, or until tender. Stir in ⅔ cup hot vegetable stock and ½ cup low-fat light cream, then toss with the drained pasta and broccoli. Season generously with salt and pepper, then pour the pasta into a large, ovenproof dish and sprinkle with 2–3 tablespoons grated mature pecorino cheese. Place in a preheated oven at 400°F and cook for 15–18 minutes, or until golden and bubbling.

30 Falafel Patties with Whole-Wheat Pita

Serves 4

2 x 13 oz cans chickpeas, drained
1 teaspoon ground cumin
1 teaspoon ground coriander
1 small red onion, finely grated
3 carrots, 1 finely grated,
    2 coarsely grated
2 garlic cloves, finely chopped
4 tablespoons finely chopped
    parsley
1 egg, lightly beaten
1 teaspoon lemon zest
4 tablespoons all-purpose flour
2 teaspoons baking powder
½ teaspoon dried red pepper
    flakes (optional)
vegetable oil, for greasing
4 warmed whole-wheat pita
    breads
7 oz low-fat tzatziki
salt and pepper

- Preheat the oven to 400°F. Place the chickpeas, cumin, and coriander in a food processor or blender and pulse until the chickpeas resemble coarse bread crumbs. Scrape into a large bowl. Add the onion, finely grated carrot, garlic, parsley, egg, lemon zest, flour, baking powder, and dried red pepper flakes. Mix until well combined.

- Lightly grease a nonstick cookie sheet and form walnut-sized spoonfuls of the mixture into 24 slightly flattened patties. Arrange on a cookie sheet and place in the oven and for 12–15 minutes, or until golden and crisp.

- Open up the warmed pitas and divide the coarsely grated carrot among the pockets, then insert the patties and drizzle over some low-fat tzatziki. Serve with more low-fat tzatziki on the side.

10 Chickpea Salad

Rinse and drain 2 x 13 oz cans chickpeas and place in a large bowl with 1 finely chopped red onion, 2 coarsely grated carrots, 4 tablespoons finely chopped parsley, 2 tablespoons chopped mint, the grated zest and juice of 1 lemon, and ½ teaspoon dried red pepper flakes. Season generously with salt and pepper and stir to combine. Spoon onto serving plates and drizzle 1 teaspoon olive oil over each. Serve with warmed whole-wheat pita breads and tzatziki.

20 Falafel Burgers

Make the falafel mixture as above and form into 8 large burgers. Heat 1 tablespoon olive oil in a large, nonstick skillet over medium heat. Cook the burgers for 7–8 minutes, or until crisp and golden, turning once. Drain on paper towels to remove any excess oil, then arrange inside warmed whole-wheat burger buns with tzatziki, chopped lettuce, and sliced tomatoes.

Watermelon, Pomegranate, and Halloumi Salad

Serves 4

7 oz low-fat halloumi cheese, cut into 8 slices

finely grated zest and juice of 1 lime

2 scallions, finely sliced

2 tablespoons chopped parsley

2 tablespoons chopped mint

1 tablespoon avocado oil

5 oz arugula

½ watermelon, peeled, seeded, and diced

½ small red onion, finely sliced

¾ cup almond-stuffed green olives

1 tablespoon pomegranate molasses

1–2 teaspoons chile paste, to taste

½ cup pomegranate seeds

pepper

- Preheat the broiler. Toss the halloumi with the lime zest, scallions, and 1 tablespoon each of the parsley and mint, then place on a foil-lined baking pan. Drizzle over a little of the avocado oil and place the pan under the broiler for 3–4 minutes until hot and golden, turning once.

- Meanwhile, divide the arugula among 4 large plates. Toss the watermelon, onion, olives, and remaining parsley and mint in a large bowl. Spoon the dressed watermelon over the arugula.

- In a small bowl, mix together the lime juice, pomegranate molasses, the remaining avocado oil, and chile paste, to taste, then season with black pepper.

- Top each salad with 2 slices of the grilled halloumi, then scatter over the pomegranate seeds. Serve drizzled with the dressing.

 Watermelon and Feta Salad

Peel, seed, and dice ½ watermelon and arrange on serving plates. Crumble 7 oz low-fat feta over the watermelon, then scatter over 2 finely sliced scallions, 2 tablespoon each of chopped mint and parsley, and ¾ cup black olives. Sprinkle over ½ cup pomegranate seeds and serve drizzled with 1 tablespoon pomegranate molasses.

Sweet Potato and Halloumi Salad with an Herb Dressing Cook 1 lb peeled sweet potatoes cut into ¾ inch slices in boiling water for 4–5 minutes to partially cook. Meanwhile, rub 1 teaspoon avocado oil over 7 oz low-fat halloumi cheese, cut into 8 slices. Heat a ridged griddle pan over medium heat, then griddle the halloumi for 3–4 minutes, turning once. Remove and set aside. Brush the parboiled sweet potato with 1 tablespoon chile oil on both sides, then griddle for 2–3 minutes each side, lifting and half-turning the pieces once to create a crisscross pattern. Meanwhile, arrange 5 oz arugula on serving plates and mix together in a small bowl 1 tablespoon each of low-fat pesto and lemon juice. Arrange the sweet potato and halloumi on the arugula, then scatter over 2 finely sliced scallions and 2 tablespoons each of chopped parsley and mint. Drizzle over the lemon dressing and serve scattered with 1 tablespoon toasted pine nuts.

30 One-Pot Southern-Style Rice

Serves 4

1½ tablespoons vegetable oil
1 large onion, chopped
2 garlic cloves, roughly chopped
1 celery stick, chopped
1 red and 1 yellow pepper, chopped
1 zucchini, chopped
1 teaspoon each dried thyme, dried
   oregano, and hot smoked paprika
¼ teaspoon cayenne pepper
1¼ cups long-grain rice, rinsed
   under cold running water
2 tablespoons tomato paste
2 x 13 oz cans chopped tomatoes
2 cups vegetable stock
salt and pepper
2 tablespoons chopped parsley
few dashes Tabasco sauce

- Heat the oil in a large Dutch oven over medium heat. Add the onion, garlic, celery, and red and yellow peppers. Cook for 4–5 minutes, stirring frequently. Then add the zucchini and cook for a further 3–4 minutes.

- Add the herbs, spices, and rice and stir-fry for 1 minute, coating the rice well in the other ingredients. Stir in the tomato paste, chopped tomatoes, and vegetable stock. Season with salt and pepper. Bring to a boil and cover with a tightly fitting lid, then reduce the heat and leave to simmer gently for 15–18 minutes, or until the rice is cooked and the mixture has thickened.

- Serve sprinkled with chopped parsley and a few dashes of Tabasco sauce, if liked.

---

10 5 Mixed-Bean and Rice Salad

Mix together a 13 oz can mixed beans, drained, a 7 oz can corn, drained, and 1¼ cups cold, steamed rice. Finely chop 1 red pepper, 1 yellow pepper, 1 celery stick, 2 scallions, and 1¼ cups quartered cherry tomatoes. Add 3 tablespoons lime juice, 2 teaspoons Tabasco sauce, 1 tablespoon vegetable oil, and 1 chopped small bunch of flat-leaf parsley and toss. Serve in bowls, topped with low-fat sour cream and toasted flour tortillas.

20 Southern-Style Mixed Vegetable and Bean Stir-Fry Chop 1 large onion, 1 celery stick, and 1 zucchini. Seed and chop 1 red and 1 yellow pepper and finely chop 2 garlic cloves. Roughly chop 2 tablespoons pickled red jalapeño peppers and set aside. Heat 1½ tablespoons vegetable oil in a large skillet or wok over medium heat, then add the raw vegetables and stir-fry for 10 minutes until tender. Add 1 teaspoon each of dried thyme, dried oregano, and hot smoked paprika and ¼ teaspoon cayenne pepper. Stir-fry for a further minute. Stir in 1½ cups steamed plain, mushroom, or chile and bean rice, then add a 13 oz can kidney beans, drained. Continue to stir-fry until hot, then divide immediately among 4 bowls, each topped with a dollop of low-fat sour cream. Scatter with chopped pickled red jalapeño peppers and serve.

 # Green Lentil Tapenade with Toast

Serves 4

8 oz ready-to-eat green Puy
lentils, rinsed and drained

2 tablespoons black olive paste

1 tablespoon caper paste or
capers, rinsed, drained, and
finely chopped

1 tablespoon lemon juice

1 cup ready-to-eat slow-roasted
tomatoes (not in oil)

2 tablespoons toasted pine nuts

½ teaspoon hot smoked paprika

salt and pepper

hot toast, to serve

- Place all of the ingredients (except the toast) in a food processor or blender and pulse to blend until smooth.

- Scrape into a bowl and serve spread over hot toast.

 ### Warm Puy Lentil Salad

In a skillet over meadium heat place 1 tablespoon olive oil. Add 3 finely chopped scallions and 2 finely chopped garlic cloves. Cook gently for 6–7 minutes, stirring. Stir in 1 tablespoon chopped capers, 1 cup chopped ready-to-eat slow-roasted tomatoes (not in oil), ½ teaspoon hot smoked paprika and 1 lb ready-to-eat cooked Puy lentils and heat through. Meanwhile, mix 2 tablespoons each of lemon and black olive paste in a small bowl, then stir into the warm salad with 3 tablespoons chopped flat-leaf parsley and salt and pepper, to taste. Serve in bowls with arugula and hot toast.

 ### Lentil and Spiced Tomato Casserole

Gently heat 1 tablespoon vegetable oil in a Dutch oven over medium-low heat. Add 1 chopped onion and 2 finely sliced garlic cloves and cook for 7–8 minutes, or until softened. Add ½ teaspoon hot smoked paprika and 1 teaspoon each of ground coriander and cumin seeds, stirring until the onion is well coated in the spices. Tip in ¼ cup Puy lentils and 1 cup roughly chopped ready-to-eat slow-roasted tomatoes (not in oil) and stir-fry for 1–2 minutes. Then add 2 tablespoons each of tomato paste and black olive paste and 3 cups of hot vegetable stock. Season generously with salt and pepper, then gently simmer for about 18 minutes or until the lentils are tender. Scatter over 1 tablespoon rinsed and drained capers and serve with hot toast.

LOW-FAST-GOH

20 Whole-Wheat Penne in a Tomato, Artichoke, and Olive Sauce

Serves 4

1 tablespoon olive oil
1 onion, finely chopped
2 garlic cloves, finely chopped
¼ cup red wine
2 x 13 oz cans chopped tomatoes
pinch of sugar
1 teaspoon finely grated lemon
  zest
1 teaspoon dried oregano
½ cup dry pitted black olives,
  roughly chopped
13 oz whole-wheat penne
1 small bunch of basil, leaves torn
13 oz can artichokes, rinsed,
  drained, and roughly chopped
salt and pepper

- Heat the olive oil in a large, heavy-based pan over medium-low heat. Add the onion and garlic and cook gently for 5–6 minutes, or until softened. Stir in the red wine, tomatoes, sugar, lemon zest, oregano, and black olives. Bring to a boil then reduce the heat and simmer gently for 12–15 minutes.

- Meanwhile, bring a large saucepan of lightly salted water to a boil and cook the pasta for 11 minutes until "al dente," or according to the package instructions.

- Add the basil and artichokes to the pasta sauce and stir until the artichokes are heated through. Season with salt and pepper.

- Drain the pasta and serve in large bowls with the pasta sauce spooned over. Serve with a green salad.

---

10 Tomato and Artichoke Bruschetta

Roughly chop 3 tomatoes and place in a bowl with 1 teaspoon dried oregano, ½ cup roughly chopped dry pitted black olives, 13 oz can artichokes, rinsed, drained, and chopped, 1 sliced scallion, 1 tablespoon lemon juice, and 1 tablespoon olive oil. Stir gently, then season with salt and pepper. Toast 4 large slices sourdough bread and rub the surface with the cut edges of 1 garlic clove. Set on serving plates, spoon over the tomato topping, and scatter with basil leaves.

30 Artichoke and Broccoli Bake

Heat 1 tablespoon olive oil in a large saucepan and fry 2 finely chopped garlic cloves over medium heat for 1 minute. Add ¼ cup red wine, 2 x 13 oz cans chopped tomatoes, a pinch of sugar, 1 teaspoon finely grated lemon zest, 1 teaspoon dried oregano, and ½ cup roughly chopped dry pitted black olives. Bring to a boil, then reduce the heat and simmer gently for 7–8 minutes. Meanwhile, cook 1 lb fresh penne pasta in a large saucepan of lightly salted boiling water with 7 oz small broccoli florets for 3–4 minutes, or until the pasta is "al dente," or according to the package instructions. Drain the pasta and broccoli, then stir into the tomato sauce. Add a 13 oz can artichokes, rinsed, drained, and roughly chopped, then scrape the mixture into an ovenproof dish. Top with a scant ½ cup ricotta in small spoonfuls. Bake in a preheated oven at 425°F for about 18 minutes or until hot and bubbling.

30 Red Quinoa with Lemon and Tomato Salad and Feta

Serves 4

¾ cup red quinoa, rinsed under cold running water

1¼ cups boiling water

4 yellow or red tomatoes, seeded and diced

1 large green pepper, finely chopped

2 scallions, finely sliced

⅔ cup pitted Kalamata olives, roughly chopped

½ cucumber, cut in half lengthways, seeded, and sliced

grated zest and juice of 1 lemon

3 tablespoons chopped parsley

3 tablespoons chopped mint

4 small Belgian endive, sliced

3½ oz low-fat feta

2 tablespoons toasted mixed seeds

small handful of alfalfa sprouts

- Tip the quinoa into a medium-sized saucepan and pour over the measured boiling water. Cover the pan and simmer gently for about 12–15 minutes. It is ready when the seed begins to come away from the germ. Drain the quinoa through a fine sieve. Cool under cold running water and drain.

- Meanwhile, mix together in a large bowl the tomatoes, pepper, scallions, olives, and cucumber, then stir in the lemon zest, parsley, and mint.

- Mix the cooled quinoa through the vegetables and season with salt, pepper, and lemon juice, to taste. Set aside for 5–10 minutes to allow the flavors to develop.

- Scatter the Belgian endive onto 4 serving plates, spoon over the quinoa salad, and crumble over the feta. Sprinkle with the toasted seeds and alfalfa sprouts and serve.

10 Minted Pea Quinoa

Heat 8 oz ready-to-eat red and white quinoa or ready-to-eat red mixed wholesome grains, according to the package instructions. Tip the quinoa or grains into a bowl and toss with 3 tablespoons each of chopped parsley and mint, 1 scant cup thawed peas, and 2 finely sliced scallions. Season with salt, pepper, and lemon juice, to taste, and crumble over 3½ oz Wensleydale cheese or a similar crumbly white cheese. Sprinkle over 2 tablespoons toasted mixed seeds and serve.

20 Spicy Pepper and Onion Quinoa

Rinse ¾ cup red quinoa under running water, then cook gently in twice its volume of boiling water for 12–15 minutes until tender. It is done when the seed begins to come away from the germ. Tip the quinoa into a fine sieve and drain away any excess water. Meanwhile, mix together the juice of 1 lemon, 1 tablespoon each of olive oil and mild harissa, and 3 tablespoons each of chopped parsley and mint. Set aside. Heat 1 tablespoon olive oil in a skillet over medium heat.

Add 1 chopped red onion, 1 seeded and finely chopped green pepper, and 2 chopped garlic cloves. Cook for 5–6 minutes, stirring occasionally, then stir in 1 teaspoon cumin seeds. When the quinoa is ready, fork through the lemon dressing, fold in the vegetables, and serve.

30 More Than 5 Vegetable Pizza

Serves 4

2 cups peeled and diced sweet
 potato
6 tablespoons thick Italian passata
2 tablespoons chopped basil
pinch of sugar
1 teaspoon dried thyme
10 oz package pizza mix
all-purpose flour, for dusting
1½ cups mushrooms, thinly sliced
1 small red pepper, thinly sliced
½ red onion, thinly sliced
½ cup frozen petit pois
2½ cups baby spinach, shredded
1 tablespoon pine nuts
1–2 tablespoons finely grated
 Parmesan cheese (optional)
salt and pepper

- Place the diced sweet potato in a pan of lightly salted boiling water and cook for 10–12 minutes until tender.

- Meanwhile, preheat the oven to 425°F. In a small bowl mix together the passata, basil, and sugar, then season with salt and pepper.

- Drain the sweet potato, then return to the pan and mash with the dried thyme. Scrape into a large bowl and stir in the package of pizza mix. Add enough warm water (about 4–6 tablespoons) to make a dough. Tip the dough out onto a lightly floured surface and knead briefly until smooth, then roll out to fit a large nonstick cookie sheet.

- Spread the passata mixture over the surface of the dough, leaving a border of ½ inch. Top with the mushrooms, red pepper, and onion, then scatter over the peas, spinach, and pine nuts. Sprinkle over the Parmesan, if using.

- Put the pizza in the oven for 12–14 minutes, or until crisp and golden. Serve with an arugula and spinach salad.

1 Mushroom, Pepper, and Onion Baguette

Subs Cut a long baguette in half, then halve lengthways to create 4 subs. Broil, cut-side up, for 1 minute. Mix 6 tablespoons thick passata, 2 tablespoons chopped basil, and a pinch of sugar. Spread over each sub. Scatter over a sliced red pepper, mushrooms, and ½ red onion, then sprinkle over 2 tablespoons grated Parmesan cheese. Broil for 5–6 minutes, then scatter over 2½ cups shredded baby spinach and 1 tablespoon pine nuts and serve.

2 Mushroom, Pepper, and Onion Calzone

Thinly slice 1½ cups mushrooms and ½ red onion. Seed and thinly slice 1 small red pepper, and roughly chop enough basil leaves to give 2 tablespoons. Pour a 10 oz package of pizza mix into a large bowl, then add enough water to make a soft dough, following the package instructions. Tip the dough onto a lightly floured surface and knead into a ball, then cut in half and roll into 2 large circles. Top half of each pizza base with the mushrooms, onion, pepper, basil, and ½ teaspoon dried thyme. Fold the uncovered dough over the vegetables and pinch down the edges to seal. Place in a preheated oven at 425°F for 10–12 minutes, or until puffed up and golden. Meanwhile, heat 6 tablespoons thick Italian passata. Remove the calzone from the oven, cut in half, pour over the warmed passata, and allow half per person. Scatter with arugula before serving.

1 ⏱ Marinated Tofu with Sesame Seeds

Serves 4

11 oz marinated tofu cubes

2 teaspoons toasted sesame
seed oil

1 lb mixed stir-fry vegetables

¼ cup rice wine or dry sherry

2 tablespoons tamari or dark
soy sauce

¼ cup mirin

1 garlic clove, finely chopped

1 teaspoon grated fresh ginger
root

1 tablespoon palm sugar or soft
light brown sugar

1 tablespoon toasted sesame
seeds

steamed Thai rice, to serve

- Pat the tofu with paper towels to remove excess oil.

- Heat the oil in wok over medium heat, then add the mixed
stir-fry vegetables. Stir-fry for 2–3 minutes, or until
starting to wilt.

- Add the tofu, rice wine, tamari or dark soy sauce, mirin, garlic,
ginger root, and sugar. Simmer for 1–2 minutes, stirring
frequently. Scatter over the sesame seeds, then serve
immediately with steamed Thai rice.

2 Marinated Tofu Salad

Cut 2 carrots, 10 radishes, and ½ seeded cucumber into matchsticks. Pat 11 oz marinated tofu cubes with paper towels. Tip the vegetable matchsticks and tofu into a bowl, then add 1½ cups bean sprouts and toss. In a separate bowl mix 1 teaspoon freshly grated ginger root, 2 tablespoons lime juice, 1 teaspoon finely grated lime zest, 1 tablespoon vegetable oil, 2 tablespoons light soy sauce, and 1 teaspoon palm sugar. Drizzle over the tofu and serve.

3 Spicy Noodle Soup with Tofu

Pour 5 cups vegetable stock into a saucepan and place over medium-high heat. Stir in ⅓ cup rice wine vinegar, 3 tablespoons dark soy sauce, 1 teaspoon freshly grated ginger root, 1 finely chopped garlic clove, 1 tablespoon palm sugar or soft light brown sugar, and 1 thinly sliced red chile. Bring to a boil, then reduce the heat and simmer gently for 18–20 minutes until fragrant. Meanwhile, cook 8 oz udon noodles in a large saucepan of boiling water for 8–10 minutes until tender, or according to the package instructions. Drain the noodles and spoon into serving bowls. Scatter 11 oz marinated tofu cubes over the noodles and ladle over the soup. Serve immediately, garnished with 2 thinly sliced scallions.

20 Lemon, Ricotta, and Zucchini Ribbons

Serves 4

13 oz small yellow and green baby
    zucchini
8 oz parpardelle or tagliatelle

Lemony ricotta

1 teaspoon fennel seeds
¼ teaspoon dried red pepper
    flakes (optional)
12–15 black peppercorns
1 cup ricotta
¼ teaspoon freshly ground
    nutmeg
finely grated zest and juice of
    1 lemon

- Bring a large saucepan of lightly salted water to a boil.

- Meanwhile, make the lemony ricotta by lightly crushing the fennel seeds with the dried red pepper flakes, if using, and black peppercorns, then tip into a bowl. Add the ricotta, nutmeg, and lemon zest and juice. Mix well, then set aside.

- Slice the zucchini thinly into ribbons using a mandolin or sharp vegetable peeler.

- Tip the pasta into the pan of boiling water and cook for 6–7 minutes until "al dente," or according to the package instructions. Two minutes before the end of cooking, add the zucchini to soften.

- Drain the pasta and zucchini, reserving 2–3 tablespoons of the cooking liquid. Return the pasta, zucchini, and reserved water to the pan, scrape in the lemony ricotta, and stir gently to combine. Season with salt and pepper, then serve immediately with a green salad.

10 Crunchy Topped Lemony Ricotta and Zucchini Bake

Make the pasta dish as above, omitting the fennel seeds from the lemony ricotta. Tip the pasta into a rectangular baking dish and sprinkle with 1¼ cups freshly made, whole-wheat bread crumbs and 1 teaspoon fennel seeds. Place under a hot broiler for 2–3 minutes until the bread crumbs are golden brown and the fennel seeds fragrant. Remove and serve immediately.

30 Lemony Ricotta Tagliatelle

Make the lemony ricotta, as above. Cook 1 lb fresh tagliatelle in lightly salted boiling water for 6–7 minutes until "al dente," or according to the package instruction. While the pasta is cooking, coarsely grate 13 oz small yellow and green baby zucchini. Drain the pasta and return to the pan over medium heat. Add the grated zucchini and lemony ricotta and stir to heat through. Serve immediately with a green salad.

LOW-FAST-DAK

30 Moroccan-Style Potato Bake

Serves 4

1½ lb baby new potatoes, halved

4 cups hot vegetable stock

1 tablespoon olive oil

1 large red onion, halved and thinly sliced

2 garlic cloves, chopped

1 preserved lemon, finely chopped

8 oz drained roasted peppers, sliced

1 teaspoon hot smoked paprika

1 teaspoon ground cumin

½ teaspoon ground ginger

2 tablespoons tomato paste

1 tablespoon aged sherry vinegar

salt and pepper

- Put the potatoes and vegetable stock in a large saucepan. Bring to a boil and cook, covered, for 12 minutes until tender but still firm.

- Meanwhile, preheat the oven to 450°F and heat the olive oil in a large, deep-sided, ovenproof skillet over medium-low heat. Add the onion and fry gently for 3–4 minutes, then add the garlic and cook for a further 3–4 minutes until softened and slightly colored.

- Stir into the onion mixture the preserved lemon, roasted peppers, the spices, tomato paste, sherry vinegar, and a little salt and pepper. Cook gently for 2 minutes.

- Drain the cooked potatoes, reserving 1¾ cups of the liquid, then add the potatoes and reserved stock to the pan. Bring up to a boil, then put the pan in oven and bake for 14–16 minutes until golden. Remove from the oven and serve immediately with a crunchy green salad.

 Pan-Fried Moroccan-Style Vegetables Roughly chop 1 lb cooked new potatoes and add to a large skillet over medium heat with 1 tablespoon olive oil, 1 teaspoon each of hot smoked paprika and ground cumin, ½ teaspoon ground ginger, 2 tablespoons tomato paste, 1 tablespoon aged sherry vinegar, 8 oz drained roasted peppers, sliced, and 1 finely chopped preserved lemon. Stir to heat through, then serve over crunchy salad greens with an extra drizzle of sherry vinegar.

 Moroccan-Style Chickpeas Cook 1 halved and thinly sliced large red onion and 2 chopped garlic cloves, as above, then add 1 teaspoon each of hot smoked paprika and ground cumin, ½ teaspoon ground ginger, 2 tablespoons tomato paste, 1 tablespoon aged sherry vinegar, 8 oz drained roasted peppers, sliced, and 1 finely chopped preserved lemon. Season with salt and pepper and cook for 1–2 minutes, then stir in 2 x 13 oz cans of rinsed and drained chickpeas. Cook for 3–4 minutes, stirring occasionally. Fold in 4 oz washed, trimmed, and roughly chopped spinach, then sprinkle over an extra 1–2 tablespoons sherry vinegar, to taste. Cook for a further 1–2 minutes until the spinach has wilted. Serve immediately.

Vietnamese-Style Vegetable Noodle Salad

Serves 4

7 oz vermicelli rice sticks

½ cucumber, seeded and cut into matchsticks

1 carrot, cut into matchsticks

1½ cups bean sprouts

1¼ cups sugar snap peas, cut into thin strips

2 tablespoons chopped cilantro

2 tablespoons chopped mint

1 red chile, seeded and finely sliced

2 tablespoons chopped blanched peanuts, to garnish

Dressing

1 tablespoon sunflower or peanut oil

½ teaspoon superfine sugar

1 tablespoon fish sauce

2 tablespoons freshly squeezed lime juice

- Bring a large saucepan of water to a boil, then turn off the heat, and add the rice sticks. Cover and leave to cook for 4 minutes until just tender, or according to the package instructions. Drain the noodles and cool immediately in a bowl of ice-cold water.

- To make the dressing, put the oil, superfine sugar, fish sauce and lime juice in a small bowl. Stir until the sugar dissolves.

- Drain the noodles and return to the bowl. Pour over half of the dressing, then tip in the vegetables, herbs, and chile. Toss until well combined.

- Heap the noodle salad on serving plates and drizzle with the remaining dressing. Serve scattered with chopped peanuts.

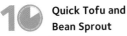

Quick Tofu and Bean Sprout Noodle Salad Make the dressing, as above. Toss 12 oz precooked rice sticks with the dressing, 1½ cups bean sprouts, 10 oz marinated tofu strips, 1 finely chopped red chile, and 2 tablespoons each of chopped cilantro and mint. Serve in deep bowls with lime wedges on the side.

Vegetable, Egg, and Noodle Stir-Fry Cook 7 oz vermicelli rice sticks and make the dressing as above, then toss half of the dressing through the noodles. In a small bowl beat together 2 eggs, 1 tablespoon soy sauce, and 2 sliced scallions. Heat 1 teaspoon peanut oil in a wok over medium-high heat, then pour in half the egg mixture. Swirl the wok to coat with the egg mixture and cook until crisp. Slide onto a plate, then repeat to make a second omelet. Roll up the omelets tightly and cut into thin shreds. Add a further teaspoon of oil to the wok over high heat. Add 2 finely sliced garlic cloves and 1 tablespoon chopped fresh ginger root and stir-fry for 30 seconds. Add 7 oz tenderstem broccoli and 5 oz thinly sliced scarlet runner beans. Stir-fry for 3–4 minutes until the vegetables are tender. Serve with the noodles, topped with the sliced omelet.

 # Meaty Mushrooms in Red Wine

Serves 4

2 garlic cloves, peeled
1 tablespoon olive oil
12 baby onions, cut in half
1 celery stick, roughly chopped
1 carrot, diced
10 oz portobello or large flat
   mushrooms, thickly sliced
7 oz button mushrooms
2 tablespoons good brandy
1 tablespoon butter
2 tablespoons all-purpose flour
1¼ cups red wine
½ teaspoon soft dark brown sugar
2 tablespoons chopped parsley,
   to garnish
salt and pepper

- Cut the garlic in half then crush with the flat side of a knife to keep whole. Heat the oil in a Dutch oven over medium-low heat. Add the garlic, onions, celery, and carrot. Cook gently for 8–10 minutes, or until golden.

- Add the mushrooms and cook for a further 5–7 minutes. Remove all the vegetables from the pan and set aside.

- Remove the pan from the heat, pour in the brandy, and carefully ignite, allowing all the alcohol to burn off. Place the pan over low heat, then add the butter and flour. Stir with a wooden spoon for 1–2 minutes. Slowly pour the red wine into the pan, stirring constantly until fully incorporated. Add the sugar and continue stirring until the sauce thickens.

- Return the vegetables to the pan and simmer gently to reheat. Season generously with salt and pepper, sprinkle with chopped parsley, and serve with mashed potatoes.

 Garlic Mushroom Open-Faced Sandwich Heat 1 tablespoon olive oil and 1 tablespoon butter in a large skillet over medium-low heat, add 2 finely chopped garlic cloves, and fry gently for 1 minute. Add 10 oz thickly sliced portobello or large flat field mushrooms to the pan and cook for 4–5 minutes until softened. Stir in ½ cup white wine and allow it to bubble for 2–3 minutes to burn off the alcohol. Stir in 2 tablespoons chopped parsley and serve on griddled or toasted bread.

 Baked Whole Mushrooms on Griddled Bread Place 4 portobello or large flat field mushrooms on a nonstick baking pan. Scatter 2 finely chopped garlic cloves over the mushrooms and season with salt and pepper. Splash a little Cognac onto each mushroom and drizzle over 1 tablespoon olive oil. Put the mushrooms in a preheated oven at 400°F for 12–15 minutes or until tender. Divide 5 oz watercress among 4 serving plates, then place a slice of griddled or toasted bread on each heap. Finish each stack with the baked mushrooms and serve immediately.

Quick Fava Bean, Pea, and Fennel Salad with Sorrel

Serves 4

1¼ cups frozen baby fava beans

1 cup frozen petit pois

1 large fennel bulb, very thinly sliced

1 teaspoon lemon juice

3½ oz sorrel leaves, washed and dried

4 sprigs mint, leaves removed and finely shredded

2–3 teaspoons avocado oil (optional)

salt and pepper

lemon wedges, to serve

- Bring a large saucepan of lightly salted water to a boil. Add the fava beans and simmer rapidly for 3 minutes, then add the peas. Bring back to a boil, then drain immediately, and tip the fava beans and peas into a bowl of ice-cold water.

- Meanwhile, toss the fennel slices with the lemon juice and season with black pepper.

- Arrange the sorrel leaves in a large serving dish, then pile the fennel on the leaves. Scatter over the peas and fava beans, and sprinkle with shredded mint leaves.

- Drizzle over the avocado oil, if using, then season with a little salt and plenty of black pepper. Serve immediately with lemon wedges.

Chilled Fennel, Fava Bean, and Pea Soup Bring a large saucepan of water to a boil, then add 1 chopped fennel bulb and cook for 5–6 minutes. Add 1¼ cups frozen baby fava beans and simmer rapidly for a further 3 minutes, then add 1 cup frozen petit pois. Bring back to a boil and cook for a further minute, then drain into a colander and cool rapidly under cold running water. Drain well and then add to 1¾ cups cold vegetable stock. Place in a blender and blitz until silky smooth. Season with salt and pepper and serve in bowls with a dollop of half-fat crème fraîche on top and garnished with mint leaves.

Warm Potato Salad with Fennel, Fava Beans, and Peas Cut 7 oz baby new potatoes in half, then cook in a saucepan of lightly salted boiling water for 10–15 minutes until tender but firm. Meanwhile, arrange 1 thinly sliced fennel bulb in a single layer on a baking pan. Spray with a little olive oil and place in a preheated oven at 400°F for 15–20 minutes or until beginning to soften. Bring a large saucepan of lightly salted water to a boil. Add 1¼ cups frozen baby fava beans and 1 cup frozen petit pois and simmer rapidly for 3 minutes, then drain. Toss the warm potatoes, fennel, fava beans, and peas with 3½ oz washed and dried sorrel leaves, scatter with the chopped leaves from 4 sprigs of mint, and serve immediately, drizzled with a little avocado oil, if liked.

30 Bean Burger with Chive and Onion Yogurt

Serves 4

13 oz can black beans
13 oz can azuki beans
1 teaspoon celery salt
2 tablespoons sun-dried tomato paste
2 teaspoons dried onion granules
1 teaspoon garlic powder
1 teaspoon ground cumin
4 tablespoons chopped cilantro
1 egg, lightly beaten
1¼ cups fresh bread crumbs
pinch of black pepper
2–3 tablespoons fine polenta or semolina, to dust
vegetable oil, for greasing
1 teaspoon cumin seeds
4 large plain or chile and jalapeño soft tortilla wraps, to serve

Chive and onion yogurt

1 cup fat-free Greek-style yogurt
½ small red onion, finely chopped
2 tablespoons chopped chives
1 tablespoon lime juice

- Preheat the oven to 425°F. Drain the beans and place in a food processor with the celery salt, tomato paste, onion granules, garlic powder, ground cumin, cilantro, egg, bread crumbs, and pepper. Pulse until the mixture is combined but not smooth. Shape into 8 burgers and dust lightly with the polenta or semolina. Place on a lightly greased cookie sheet and bake in the oven for 10–12 minutes, turning once, until cooked and crisp.

- Meanwhile, to make the chive and onion yogurt, mix together the yogurt, onion, chives, and lime juice and season with salt and pepper. Cover with plastic wrap and chill in the fridge.

- Heat a small skillet over medium heat and dry-roast the cumin seeds, stirring, until fragrant. Then set aside to cool.

- Heat a ridged griddle pan over medium-high heat and toast one side of a tortillas until lightly charred but not brittle. Fold into quarters, set aside, and then repeat with the remaining tortillas. Scatter the cumin seeds over the chive and onion yogurt.

- When ready to serve, place 2 burgers inside each folded tortilla. Spoon in some chive and onion yogurt and serve with any remaining yogurt in a bowl on the side.

---

10 Black Bean Pâté

Put a 13 oz can black beans, drained, in a food processor with 5 oz can drained chickpeas, 4 tablespoons chopped cilantro, 1 tablespoon lime juice, 2 teaspoons dried onion, and 1 teaspoon each of celery salt, garlic powder, and ground cumin. Pulse to a smooth-textured pâté, then season with salt and pepper. Spread on hot toast to serve.

20 Chili Bean Wraps

Mix together in a large bowl 13 oz can black beans, drained, 13 oz can azuki beans, drained, 1 seeded and finely chopped red pepper, 4 tablespoons finely chopped cilantro, 2 tablespoons sun-dried tomato paste, 2 teaspoons dried onion, and 1 teaspoon each of celery salt, garlic powder, and ground cumin. Spoon the mixture on 4 plain or chile and jalapeño soft tortilla wraps. Roll them up firmly and place in a snug-fitting ovenproof dish. Pour over 10 oz spicy tomato salsa, then place in a preheated oven at 425°F for 15 minutes, or until hot. Serve with shredded iceberg lettuce and top each plate with a spoonful of low-fat sour cream.

30 Grilled Vegetable Salad

Serves 4

7 oz button mushrooms
1 red pepper, cut into quarters
1 green pepper, cut into quarters
1 onion, sliced ½ inch thick
2 long green chiles
1 tablespoon olive oil
3 tomatoes, chopped
13 oz can chickpeas
2 hard-cooked eggs, chopped
½ cup black olives
salt and pepper

Harissa dressing

1 tablespoon olive oil
3 tablespoons chopped flat-leaf
 parsley
3 tablespoons chopped mint
½ teaspoon ground coriander
½ teaspoon ground cumin
2 tablespoons lemon juice
1 teaspoon harissa

- Preheat the broiler. Toss the mushrooms, red and green peppers, onion, and chiles with the olive oil and season generously with salt and pepper. Spread out the vegetables on a large nonstick baking pan and cook under the broiler for 4–5 minutes each side until charred and almost tender. Then tip onto a cutting board.

- When the vegetables are cool enough to handle, chop into bite-size pieces and set aside to cool further.

- To make the harissa dressing, mix all the dressing ingredients in a small bowl until well combined and set aside.

- Put the chopped vegetables, tomatoes, drained chickpeas, and dressing in a large bowl and toss until well combined. Spoon the salad onto serving plates and top with the chopped hard-cooked egg and black olives.

 Moroccan-Style Vegetable Salad

Finely chop 1 green and 1 red pepper, 1 onion, 2 long green chiles, and 3 tomatoes. Mix the chopped vegetables with 2 tablespoons each of olive oil, red wine vinegar, 1 teaspoon harissa, and 3 tablespoons each of chopped flat-leaf parsley and mint. Season with salt and pepper and serve topped with 2 chopped hard-cooked eggs and ½ cup black olives with torn pieces of griddled flatbreads on the side.

 Vegetable Skewers with Harissa

Dressing Seed and chop into bite-size chunks 1 green and 1 red pepper. Chop 1 onion into bite-size pieces. Put the peppers and onion in a large bowl with 7 oz button mushrooms, then toss with 2 tablespoons olive oil. Season with salt and pepper, then thread the vegetables onto 4 long metal skewers and place on a broiler pan. Slide the pan under a preheated broiler and cook the vegetables for 8–10 minutes, or until tender and lightly charred, turning frequently. Meanwhile, make the harissa dressing as above. Serve the vegetable skewers with steamed couscous or bulghur wheat, drizzled with the harissa dressing.

30 Lemony Pea and Ricotta Risotto

Serves 4

1½ tablespoons canola oil
4 sweet shallots, chopped
1 garlic clove, finely chopped
1¼ cups risotto rice
½ cup dry vermouth
5 cups hot vegetable stock
2 cups frozen peas, defrosted
finely grated zest of 1 lemon
1½ tablespoons lemon juice
½ cup ricotta
salt and pepper

To serve

finely grated Parmesan cheese
(optional)
lemon wedges

- Place the oil in a large, deep-sided skillet over medium-low heat. Add the shallots and garlic, and cook gently for 4–5 minutes until softened. Pour in the risotto rice and stir for a minute until the grains are coated in oil.

- Add the vermouth to the pan with the risotto rice and simmer rapidly, stirring constantly, until the liquid is absorbed. Reduce the heat slightly and add a small ladleful of the hot vegetable stock, stirring constantly at a gentle simmer, until the stock is absorbed. Repeat this process until all of the stock is absorbed and the rice is "al dente"—about 17 minutes.

- Stir in the peas, lemon zest and juice, and the ricotta. Season generously with salt and pepper. Stir over the heat until warmed through, then remove, cover, and set aside to rest for 2–3 minutes.

- Serve the risotto sprinkled with grated Parmesan, if liked, and lemon wedges.

 Lemony Stir-Fried Rice with Ricotta
Place 1 tablespoon canola oil in a skillet over medium heat. Add 4 chopped shallots and cook for 3–4 minutes, or until softened. Add 2 cups defrosted frozen peas, 7 oz can corn, drained, 2¾ cups plain steamed rice, and the finely grated zest of 1 lemon. Stir to heat through, then season generously with salt and pepper. Spoon into serving bowls. Top each bowl with a spoonful of ricotta and drizzle with a little lemon juice to serve.

 Spaghetti with Lemony Pea and Ricotta Pesto Cook 13 oz spaghetti in a large saucepan of lightly salted boiling water for 11 minutes until "al dente," or according to the package instructions. Meanwhile, cook 2 cups defrosted frozen peas for 2–3 minutes or until just tender in a saucepan of lightly salted boiling water. Drain, reserving 2 tablespoons of the cooking liquid. Tip half of the peas and the reserved cooking liquid into a food processor bowl or blender with 1 tablespoon toasted pine nuts, ½ finely chopped garlic, the chopped leaves of 1 small bunch of basil, the finely grated zest of 1 lemon, 2 tablespoons lemon juice, and 4 tablespoons ricotta. Pulse until almost smooth, then season generously with salt and pepper. Drain the pasta and toss with the pea pesto and the remaining cooked peas. Serve immediately.

LOW-FAST-QIT

Creamy Stuffed Roast Peppers with Mixed Grains

Serves 4

4 long red peppers, halved lengthwise and seeded

¼ cup chopped walnut pieces

1 lb ready-to-eat mixed wholesome grains

2 tablespoons lemon juice

2 tablespoons sun-dried tomato paste

3 tablespoons chopped mixed herbs, such as parsley, tarragon, chives, and thyme

salt and pepper

Cheese filling

1⅓ cups extra-light cream cheese

3 tablespoons chopped mixed herbs, such as parsley, tarragon, chives, and thyme

1 teaspoon grated lemon zest

2 tablespoons toasted mixed seeds

- Preheat the oven to 400°F.

- To make the cheese filling, mix together all the ingredients in a small bowl and season with salt and pepper.

- Place the pepper halves on a baking pan and spoon the filling into them. Then scatter over the walnuts. Cook the stuffed peppers in the oven for 12–15 minutes until tender and the filling is golden.

- Meanwhile, warm the mixed grains in a large pan, or according to the package instructions. Toss with the lemon juice, tomato paste, and mixed herbs, then season with salt and pepper.

- Spoon the seasoned mixed grains onto serving plates, arrange the stuffed peppers on top, and serve immediately.

---

1 Grilled Red Pepper and Cream Cheese Rolls with Mixed Grain Salad

Make the cheese filling as above. Spread the filling over 14½ oz well-drained, large, grilled red peppers halves and roll up tightly. Mix together 1 lb cold, ready-to-eat wholesome mixed grains, 2 tablespoons lemon juice, 3 tablespoons chopped mixed herbs as above, 1 tablespoon sun-dried tomato paste, and 3 oz arugula and serve with the pepper rolls.

3 Creamy Red Pepper Pasta Bake

Cook 1 lb fresh fusilli in lightly salted boiling water for 3–4 minutes until "al dente," or according to the package instructions. Make the cheese filling as above, then beat in 1 lb sieved passata. Stir the pasta into the tomato sauce, then scrape the pasta and sauce into an ovenproof dish. Mix 3 tablespoons chopped mixed herbs as above with 1 cup fresh bread crumbs and scatter over the pasta. Bake in a preheated oven at 400°F for 18–20 minutes until crisp and hot.

LOW-FAST-QUA

30 Broccoli and Baby Corn Stir-Fry with Oyster Sauce

Serves 4

2 teaspoons sesame seed oil

2 garlic cloves, thinly sliced

1 tablespoon chopped fresh
  ginger root

1 red chile, seeded and finely
  chopped

2 scallions, thickly sliced

1 teaspoon salt

4 oz baby corn

10 oz broccoli rabe

4 tablespoons oyster sauce

2 tablespoons light soy sauce

2 teaspoons toasted sesame seeds

Ginger and lemon grass rice

1 lemon grass stalk

1½ cups Thai jasmine rice, rinsed
  2–3 times

1 tablespoon chopped fresh
  ginger root

1 teaspoon salt

3 cups water

- Make the ginger and lemon grass rice by removing and discarding the outer leaves of the lemon grass. Finely slice the tender heart. Place in a saucepan with the rice, ginger root, and salt. Add the measured water and bring to a boil. Reduce the heat, cover the pan with a tightly fitting lid, and simmer gently for 14–16 minutes, or until the rice is sticky and tender and the water is absorbed. Set aside.

- When you are ready to eat, prepare the stir-fry. Heat the oil in a large wok over a medium heat, then add garlic, ginger root, chile, and scallions. Stir-fry for 30 seconds. Add the baby corn and broccoli rabe and stir-fry for 3–4 minutes, or until almost tender. Then stir in the oyster sauce and light soy sauce and simmer gently for 30 seconds.

- Remove the stir-fry from the heat and serve with the ginger and lemon grass rice with the sesame seeds sprinkled over.

 Chow Mein Stir-Fry
Cook 13 oz medium egg noodles in lightly salted boiling water for 3–4 minutes until tender, or according to the package instructions. Meanwhile, cook the stir-fry, as above. Drain the noodles into a colander, and when the vegetables are tender add to the wok. Pour over 7 oz chow mein stir-fry sauce and stir until it is heated through Serve immediately.

 Stir-Fried Vegetables with Black Bean Sauce Place 1½ cups Thai jasmine rice, rinsed 2–3 times, in a saucepan with 1 teaspoon salt and 3 cups water. Bring to a boil, reduce the heat, cover the pan with a lid, and simmer gently for 14–16 minutes, or until the rice is sticky and tender and the water is absorbed. Meanwhile, tip a 13 oz can of rinsed and drained black beans into a food processor or blender with 1 teaspoon each of finely chopped garlic and finely grated fresh ginger root, 2 tablespoons light soy sauce, 1 tablespoon oyster sauce, and 1 teaspoon sugar. Pulse to mix but not to a puree. Stir-fry the vegetables, as above, then stir in the black bean sauce and simmer for 1–2 minutes until heated through. Stir in the rice and serve immediately.

LOW-FAST-CEW

Mediterranean Bowl of Giant Couscous

Serves 4

1 vegetable stock cube

5 oz giant couscous

1¾ cups mixed cherry tomatoes

6 oz drained roasted red peppers, chopped

½ cucumber, seeded and chopped

1 small bunch of basil leaves

13 oz can chickpeas, drained

1 small bunch of flat-leaf parsley, chopped

2 scallions, finely chopped

3½ oz low-fat feta

salt and pepper

Dressing

2 oz roasted red peppers

2 tablespoons lime juice

2 tablespoons aged balsamic syrup

1 teaspoon chipotle or chile paste

¼ teaspoon garlic puree

- Bring a large saucepan of water to a boil, then stir in the vegetable stock cube. Add the couscous to the pan and cook for 6–8 minutes until "al dente," or according to the package instructions. Drain into a large, fine sieve and cool under cold running water.

- Meanwhile, quarter the tomatoes and mix with the peppers, cucumber, basil, and chickpeas in a large bowl. Make the dressing by putting all the ingredients in a mini chopper or a small food processor bowl and blending until smooth.

- Mix the cooled couscous with the vegetables and chickpeas, then stir in half of the dressing and toss until all the ingredients are well coated. Season with salt and pepper, then divide into serving bowls.

- Mix together the parsley and scallions, scatter over each bowl of couscous, and then crumble over the feta. Serve with Mediterranean-style flatbread and the remaining dressing, if liked.

10 Quick Mediterranean Couscous Salad

Cook, drain, and cool 5 oz giant couscous as above. Meanwhile, cut 1¾ cups mixed cherry tomatoes into quarters. When the couscous is cold, stir in 2 x 9 oz jars mixed antipasti, rinsed well and drained, and the tomatoes. Toss through 1 shredded small bunch of basil, 1 chopped small bunch of flat-leaf parsley, and 2 finely chopped scallions until well combined. Season with salt and pepper and serve.

30 Mediterranean Tomato and Orzo Soup

Heat 1 tablespoon olive oil in a large skillet over medium heat. Add 1 chopped large red onion and 3 finely chopped garlic cloves. Cook for 5–6 minutes until softened. Add 1¾ cups quartered mixed cherry tomatoes, 6 oz drained and chopped pimiento piquillo or roasted red peppers, the shredded leaves of 1 small bunch of basil, 1 chopped small bunch of flat-leaf parsley, 4 cups hot vegetable stock, and 1 lb sieved passata. Bring to a boil, then stir in 7 oz orzo. Reduce the heat and simmer for 20 minutes, or until the soup is thick and chunky and the orzo tender. Serve with Mediterranean flatbread, if liked.

LOW-FAST-FUX

QuickCook

Healthy
Desserts

Recipes listed by cooking by time

10

Individual Baked Strawberry and Lemon Meringues

Serves 4

2 cups strawberries, hulled and roughly chopped

1 teaspoon finely grated lemon zest

1–2 teaspoon maple syrup or liquid honey, to taste

½ teaspoon vanilla bean paste or extract

2 teaspoons finely chopped mint (optional)

1 large egg white

¼ cup superfine sugar

- Preheat the oven to 400°F. Put the strawberries, lemon zest, maple syrup, vanilla bean paste, and chopped mint in a bowl and toss until all the ingredients are well combined. Spoon the strawberries and any juice into 4 ramekins or other small ovenproof dishes.

- Place the egg white in a large, clean bowl and use an electric hand mixer to whisk into firm peaks. Add the sugar, a tablespoon at a time, whisking constantly, until all the sugar has been incorporated.

- Spoon the raw meringue mixture over the fruit in a high peak, then bake in the oven for 5–7 minutes, or until pale golden. Remove from the oven and serve immediately.

10 Strawberry, Lemon, and Vanilla Cream

Tartlets Prepare the strawberry mixture as above. Beat together 1 tablespoon vanilla sugar, 2 tablespoons lemon curd, and 1 cup fat-free Greek-style yogurt in a small bowl until well combined. Spoon the mixture into 4 small pastry tartlet cases. Arrange the prepared strawberries over the cream and serve immediately.

30 Boozy Amaretto Strawberry

Meringues Place 3 cups hulled strawberries in a small saucepan with 1 teaspoon finely grated lemon zest, 1–2 teaspoons maple syrup or honey, to taste, ½ teaspoon vanilla extract, and 2 tablespoons Amaretto liqueur. Put the pan over medium heat and warm the ingredients gently for 5–6 minutes or until the strawberries begin to collapse. Spoon the strawberries into 4 ramekins, reserving any excess liquid. Place 1 large egg white in a roomy, clean bowl and use an electric hand mixer to whisk into firm peaks. Add ¼ cup superfine sugar, a tablespoon at a time, whisking constantly, until all the sugar has been incorporated. Spoon the raw meringue over the strawberries and bake in a preheated oven at 400°F for 5–7 minutes, or until pale golden. Serve immediately with the reserved cooking liquid.

Poached Apricots with Orange Flower Water and Pistachio Nuts

Serves 4

13 oz ready-to-eat semidried apricots

1½ cups apple and elderflower juice

2 tablespoons orange flower water

½ teaspoon ground cinnamon

2 tablespoons liquid honey

½ cup shelled unsalted pistachio nuts, crushed

- Put the apricots in a pan with the apple and elderflower juice, orange flower water, cinnamon, and honey. Bring to a gentle boil over medium-high heat. Reduce the heat and simmer for 2–3 minutes until fragrant.

- Pour the apricots and juices into a large bowl and set aside to cool slightly.

- Serve in deep bowl, scattered with the pistachio nuts.

 Poached Apricots with Scented Yogurt Place 12–16 whole apricots, 2 cups water, 1½ cups apple and elderflower juice, 2 tablespoons orange flower water, 1 teaspoon vanilla bean paste or extract, and 2 tablespoons liquid honey in a saucepan over medium-high heat. Bring to a gentle boil. Reduce the heat and simmer gently for 10–12 minutes. Meanwhile, beat together 2 teaspoons orange flower water and ¾ cup fat-free Greek-style yogurt in a bowl. Spoon the poached apricots into bowls with as much of the cooking liquid as desired. Serve with the scented yogurt and thin almond cookies.

 Apricot and Pistachio Puff Pastry Slices Cut a 7½ oz sheet of ready-rolled puff pastry into quarters to make 4 rectangles, 5½ x 4 inches. Arrange the pastry rectangles on a lightly greased, nonstick baking pan and place 2 drained apricot halves in juice, cut-side down, over each pastry rectangle. In a bowl, mix 2 tablespoons orange flower water, ½ teaspoon ground cinnamon, and 2 tablespoons liquid honey. Brush the mixture over the apricots and bake in a preheated oven at 400°F for 15–18 minutes, or until the pastry is golden and crisp. Roughly chop ½ cup shelled unsalted pistachio nuts, scatter over the pastry slices, and serve.

LOW-HEAL-WIB

30 Fresh Berries with Crunchy Oats

Serves 4

1 lb mixed berries, such as black and red currants, blueberries, strawberries, raspberries, and blackberries

1 teaspoon orange blossom water

¼ teaspoon mixed spice

1–2 tablespoons soft dark brown sugar (optional)

1½ cups crunchy oat cereal, such as almond and raisin

- Preheat the oven to 350°F. Wash and hull the fresh berries, if necessary.

- Place the berries in a large bowl with the orange blossom water, mixed spice, and sugar, if using, and toss until well combined. Tip the coated fruits into an ovenproof dish, then sprinkle over the oat cereal, pressing down to flatten.

- Bake in the oven for 18–20 minutes, or until golden and crisp, remove from the oven, and serve immediately.

10 Summer Fruit Compote with Crunchy Oat Topping

Spoon 2 cups fat-free Greek-style yogurt into 4 glass dishes. Top with 1 lb pureed compote, such as summer fruits or rhubarb and strawberry, and spoon over 1½ cups crunchy oat cereal, such as almond and raisin. Serve immediately.

20 Quick Frozen Summer Fruit

Mini Pavlovas Whip ½ cup low-fat whipping cream to soft peaks and set aside. Put in a blender or food processor 8 oz frozen summer fruits, 2 tablespoons liquid honey, and ½ cup cranberry juice. Blend until just smooth but still very thick. Spoon the iced fruit mixture onto 4 ready-made meringue nests and top each with a large dollop of whipped cream. Drizzle 1 tablespoon blackcurrant or raspberry coulis over each pavlova and serve immediately.

20 Sweet and Sour Spiced Pineapple and Mango

Serves 4

1 firm, ripe mango

1 small pineapple, sliced in half lengthways and then into thin wedges

2 tablespoons confectioner's sugar, plus extra to serve

Sweet and sour dressing

½ long red chile, seeded and finely chopped

4 tablespoons lime juice

2 tablespoons palm sugar or soft light brown sugar

1–2 tablespoons finely shredded mint leaves

- Heat a ridged griddle pan over medium-high heat.

- Cut 2 sides from the mango, using the seed as a guide and cutting either side of it. Sift confectioner's sugar all over the cut sides of the mango and pineapple until well covered.

- Lay the mango, cut-side down, and pineapple on the hot pan and griddle for 2 minutes, lifting and giving the pieces a half- turn once so that a charred crisscross pattern appears on the cooked surface. Flip the pineapple wedges over and repeat on the other side. You may need to do this in 2 batches.

- Meanwhile, make the sweet and sour dressing. Put the chile, lime juice, sugar, and mint in a small bowl, then stir until the sugar is dissolved. Set aside.

- Remove the fruits from the griddle pan and arrange on serving plates. Drizzle over the sweet and sour dressing and serve dusted with extra confectioner's sugar, if liked.

 Fruit Skewers with Sweet and Sour Dressing Seed, peel, and cut into rough chunks 1 firm, ripe mango. Peel and cut into rough chunks 1 small, ripe pineapple. Hull 12 small strawberries. Thread the fruit pieces onto 8 wooden skewers and arrange on plates. Make the sweet and sour dressing as above, then pour the dressing over the chopped fruit. Serve immediately or leave to marinate for an hour before serving, if desired.

 Sticky Baked Chile Mango and Pineapple Seed, peel, and slice 1 ripe mango and peel and slice 1 small, ripe pineapple. Arrange the fruit pieces over the base of a shallow, nonstick roasting pan. Scatter ½ seeded and finely chopped long red chile over the fruit, then sprinkle with 2 tablespoons palm sugar or soft light brown sugar and drizzle over 4 tablespoons lime juice. Put the roasting pan in a preheated oven at 350°F for 15–20 minutes, or until the fruit is tender. Serve immediately, drizzled with the sticky juices and decorated with mint leaves.

30 Lemon Yogurt Cupcakes

Makes 12

½ cup peanut oil
½ cup fat-free plain yogurt
2 eggs, lightly beaten
1 teaspoon finely grated lemon zest
1/3 cup golden superfine sugar
1¼ cups all-purpose flour
½ cup ground almonds
1 teaspoon baking powder
½ teaspoon baking soda
pinch of salt

- Preheat the oven to 350°F and line a 12-cup cupcake or muffin pan with small silicone or paper bake cases.

- Put all the ingredients in a large bowl and beat until smooth, then spoon the batter into the bake cases. Bake the cakes in the oven for 18 minutes, or until risen, golden, and firm to the touch.

- Remove from the oven and transfer the cupcakes to a wire rack. Serve warm or cold.

10 Creamy Lemon Yogurt Mousse

Beat together 1 teaspoon finely grated lemon zest, 1¼ cups fat-free Greek-style yogurt with honey, ½ cup low-fat cream cheese, and 1–2 tablespoons superfine sugar, to taste. Spoon the mixture into 4 ramekin dishes and serve sprinkled with 2 oz crushed amaretti cookies.

20 Blueberry and Lemon Spongecake

Dessert Lay 4 small slices of lemon spongecake on a cutting board and cut out 4 rounds, about 2½ inches in diameter, to fit inside the bottom of 4 similar-sized ramekins. Place a cake disk into the bottom of each ramekin and top with 1 cup blueberries. Beat together 1¼ cups fat-free Greek-style yogurt with liquid honey, 1 teaspoon finely grated lemon zest, 2 teaspoons lemon juice, and ½ cup ground almonds in a bowl. Spoon the mixture over the blueberries, then sprinkle 1 teaspoon golden superfine sugar over each one. Place under a preheated broiler for 2–3 minutes until the sugar has dissolved. Remove and set aside to cool slightly, then serve.

LOW-HEAL-SIE

 Blueberry and Orange Eton Mess

Serves 4

1 cup low-fat fresh chilled
   custard
¾ cup fat-free blueberry yogurt
1 teaspoon finely grated orange
   zest
1 teaspoon vanilla bean paste or
   extract
1 cup blueberries
4 ready-made meringues nests,
   about 2 oz total weight

- Put the custard, yogurt, orange zest, and vanilla bean paste or extract in a bowl. Stir until well combined.

- Put two-thirds of the blueberries in 4 tall glasses. Spoon over the blueberry yogurt mixture, then top each glass with a lightly crushed meringue. Sprinkle over the remaining blueberries and serve immediately.

 Blueberry Compote Eton Mess

Put 1 cup blueberries, the seeds scraped from 1 vanilla pod, 1 teaspoon finely grated orange zest, and 2–3 tablespoons freshly squeezed orange juice, to taste, in a small saucepan. Place over high heat and bring to a boil. Reduce the heat and simmer gently for 5 minutes. Remove from the heat, then pour into a bowl and place the bowl inside a larger bowl filled ice cubes and cold water. Set aside to cool. Meanwhile, whip ⅔ cup low-fat whipping cream, then fold in 4 crushed ready-made meringues, about 2 oz total weight. Gently fold half the blueberries into the meringue mix, then spoon into serving dishes. Drizzle the remaining blueberry mixture over the top and serve.

 Individual Baked Blueberry Flans

Spread 4 tablespoons reduced-sugar blueberry jam over 4 individual spongecakes. Spoon 1 cup blueberries on top of the jam and set aside. Place 1 large egg white in a clean, roomy bowl and use an electric hand mixer to whisk into firm peaks. Add ¼ cup vanilla sugar, a tablespoon at a time, whisking constantly, until all the sugar has been incorporated. Whisk in 1 teaspoon finely grated orange zest, then spoon the mixture over the spongecakes and level the surface. Place the flans in a preheated oven at 400°F for 5–6 minutes, or until starting to turn golden. Remove from the oven and serve immediately with chilled custard, if desired.

30 Individual Chocolate Pots

Serves 4

3½ tablespoons melted butter, plus extra for greasing

⅔ cup all-purpose flour

1 teaspoon baking powder

1 tablespoon dark cocoa powder

¼ cup ground almonds

¼ cup soft dark brown sugar

1 egg, lightly beaten

¼ cup lowfat milk

¾ raspberries, to serve

- Preheat the oven to 350°F. Lightly grease 4 ramekins, ¾ cup each in size, and set aside. Sift together the flour, baking powder, and cocoa powder into a large bowl. Stir in the ground almonds and sugar.

- Beat the egg with the milk and melted butter in a small bowl, then pour into the dry ingredients and stir until combined.

- Spoon the mixture into the pudding bowls and bake in the oven for 15 minutes, or until risen and firm to the touch.

- Meanwhile, lightly whip the cream to soft peaks.

- Serve the chocolate pots warm with fresh raspberries.

10 Warm Pancakes with Raspberries and Melted Chocolate

Melt 3½ oz semisweet chocolate in a small bowl over a pan of barely simmering water. Toast 8 mini buttermilk pancakes under a preheated broiler for 1–2 minutes, turning once, and place 2 pancakes on each serving plate. Scatter over 2 cups fresh raspberries, then drizzle each plate with the melted chocolate. Serve warm, scattered with 2 tablespoons lightly crushed toasted hazelnuts, if desired.

20 Mint Chocolate Dipped Strawberries

Melt 5 oz good-quality, mint-flavored chocolate in a small bowl over a pan of barely simmering water. Completely cover a large cutting board or cookie sheet with plastic wrap. Dip the tips of 20 large strawberries into the melted chocolate and place on the prepared board or sheet. Place in the fridge to chill for 12–15 minutes. Serve when the chocolate has set.

LOW-HEAL-KEG

20 Cinnamon and Raisin Pear Trifle

Serves 4

6 oz panettone, cut into bite-size
   cubes
⅔ cup raisins
1 teaspoon cinnamon
13 oz can pears in juice
⅓ cup hazelnuts
1 lb low-fat fresh vanilla custard
4 tablespoons lowfat crème
   fraîche

- Place the panettone in the bottom of 4 glass serving dishes.

- Put the raisins, half of the cinnamon, and ½ cup of the juice from the pears in a saucepan over medium-high heat and bring up to a gentle boil. Reduce the heat and simmer for a minute, then turn off the heat and set aside for 5 minutes.

- Meanwhile, heat a skillet over medium heat, put the hazelnuts in the pan, and dry-roast until golden. Remove from the pan and crush lightly.

- Beat the custard with the remaining ½ teaspoon cinnamon in a bowl and slice the pears into thick pieces.

- Pour the warm raisin mixture over the panettone cubes and cover with the sliced pears. Pour over the custard and place in the refrigerator for 8–10 minutes.

- Spoon 1 tablespoon of the crème fraîche over each trifle and serve scattered with the crushed toasted hazelnuts.

10 Quick Raspberry and Pear Trifle

Cube 4 large slices of pound cake and place in the bottom of a large glass bowl. Roughly chop 13 oz can pears in juice and add to the glass bowl with 7 oz raspberry coulis. Stir all the ingredients gently to just combine. Fold 4 tablespoons half-fat crème fraîche into 1 lb low-fat fresh vanilla custard in a bowl, then spoon over the cake and fruit mix. Sprinkle with 2 tablespoons chopped toasted nuts and serve.

30 Raisin Bread and Butter Pudding

Cut 4 large slices of cinnamon and raisin bread into triangles and layer into 4 large, shallow, lightly buttered ovenproof serving dishes. Scatter over ⅔ cup raisins. Beat 2 large eggs, ¾ cup lowfat milk, ½ cup fat-free Greek-style yogurt, and 3 tablespoons soft light brown sugar in a jug, then pour the mixture over the raisins and bread. Place the dishes in a large roasting pan and add boiling water until the water comes halfway up the sides of the dishes. Bake in a preheated oven at 350°F for 20–25 minutes or until the custard is just set. Remove from the oven and serve each dish dusted with 1 teaspoon cinnamon sugar or Demerara sugar.

LOW-HEAL-WUM

3 Baked Figs with Dessert Wine Syrup

Serves 4

6–8 fresh figs, depending on size, cut in half lengthways

½ cup Sauternes dessert wine

2 tablespoons liquid honey

pinch of saffron threads

2 tablespoons flaked almonds

4 scoops low-fat vanilla ice cream, to serve (optional)

- Preheat the oven to 350°F. Lay the figs, cut-side down, in a snugly fitting ovenproof dish. Mix together the Sauternes, honey, and saffron threads in a jug or bowl and pour over the figs. Put the figs in the oven for 15–18 minutes, or until tender.

- Meanwhile, heat a small skillet over medium heat, add the flaked almonds, and dry-roast until just golden. Tip onto a plate to cool.

- Remove the figs from the oven and leave to cool for 5 minutes before serving. Transfer the figs to serving plates, drizzle with the dessert wine syrup, and scatter with the toasted almonds. Add a scoop of vanilla ice cream, if desired, and serve.

---

1 Syrupy Pan-Fried Figs Cut 6–8 fresh figs, depending on size, in half lengthways. Melt 2 tablespoons butter in a large skillet over medium heat, and lay the figs, cut-side down, in the pan. Increase the heat to high and cook the figs for 2–3 minutes until lightly colored. Turn over the figs and add ½ cup Sauternes dessert wine, 2 tablespoons honey, and a pinch of saffron threads. Bring to a gentle boil, then reduce the heat and simmer gently for 6–8 minutes or until tender. Cool slightly, then serve the figs with the syrupy liquid drizzled over and scattered with 2 tablespoons toasted flaked almonds.

2 Figs with Ricotta and Dessert Wine Syrup Put ½ cup Sauternes dessert wine, 2 tablespoons honey, and a pinch of saffron threads in a small pan over medium-high heat and bring to a gentle boil. Reduce the heat and simmer gently for 5–6 minutes to reduce the liquid by about half. Meanwhile, cut 6–8 ripe figs, depending on size, into quarters and arrange in serving dishes. Top each bowl with 1 tablespoon ricotta. Drizzle over the warm syrup and serve.

1 Quick Spiced Rhubarb and Ginger Fool

Serves 4

¾ cup fat-free Greek-style yogurt
¾ cup low-fat fromage frais
½ teaspoon ground ginger
pinch of ground cinnamon
2 pieces of stem ginger in syrup, finely chopped
2 tablespoons ginger cordial
13 oz rhubarb or rhubarb and strawberry compote
4 oz amaretti cookies, lightly crushed

- Beat together the yogurt, fromage frais, ground ginger, cinnamon, and stem ginger in a large bowl.

- Stir the ginger cordial into the rhubarb or rhubarb and strawberry compote. Then, using a large metal spoon, gently fold the compote into the spiced yogurt.

- Spoon half of the mixture into 4 attractive glass serving dishes and scatter over almost all the crushed amaretti cookies. Top with the remaining fool mixture, then finish with a scant scattering of biscuits, to decorate. Serve immediately.

2 Rhubarb, Orange, and Ginger Fool

Place 1 lb freshly chopped rhubarb, 4 tablespoons light soft brown sugar, 2 teaspoons finely grated orange zest, 2 tablespoons ginger cordial, and 2 finely chopped pieces of stem ginger in syrup in a saucepan. Stir gently over low heat to dissolve the sugar, then bring up to a gentle simmer. Cook the rhubarb for 10 minutes, or until tender. Meanwhile, beat ½ teaspoon ground ginger, a pinch of ground cinnamon, and 1 tablespoon stem ginger syrup into ¾ cup fat-free Greek-style yogurt mixed with ¾ cup low-fat fromage frais. Place the cooked rhubarb in a blender and blend until smooth. Spoon into deep bowls, top with the spiced yogurt and fromage frais mixture and 6 crushed ginger nut cookies, and serve.

3 Baked Spiced Rhubarb with Yogurt

Place 1 lb freshly chopped rhubarb into a bowl with ½ teaspoon ground ginger, a pinch of ground cinnamon, 4 tablespoons soft light brown sugar, 1 teaspoon vanilla bean paste, 1 teaspoon finely grated orange zest, and 2 tablespoons ginger cordial. Mix well, tip into an ovenproof dish, and place in a preheated oven at 400°F for 20–25 minutes, stirring occasionally until the rhubarb is tender. Serve hot with dollops of fat-free Greek-style yogurt and 8 Italian-style biscotti.

Crêpes with Vanilla Blueberries

Serves 4

1¾ cups blueberries

2 tablespoons freshly squeezed orange juice

1–2 tablespoons vanilla sugar, to taste

vegetable oil, for greasing

4 tablespoons half-fat crème fraîche, to serve (optional)

Crêpe mix

1 cup all-purpose flour

1 egg

1¼ cups lowfat milk

- Put the crêpe ingredients into a blender and process until smooth. Leave to rest for 10 minutes.

- Meanwhile, place the blueberries, orange juice, and vanilla sugar, to taste, in a small saucepan over low heat. Warm the mixture gently until the blueberries begin to burst. Remove from the heat and set aside to cool slightly.

- Heat a small, nonstick crêpe pan or small skillet over medium heat and grease the surface lightly with a little vegetable oil. Pour a little batter into the pan and swirl to coat thinly; the mixture should make 8 crêpes in total. Cook gently for 2 minutes or until golden underneath, then flip over the crêpe and cook on the other side for about 30 seconds. Slide onto a plate, cover with a piece of parchment paper and repeat the process to make the remaining crêpes.

- To serve, fold 2 crêpes onto each warmed serving plate and spoon over the warm vanilla blueberries. Serve with a dollop of half-fat crème fraîche, if desired.

---

1 Quick Vanilla-Sugar Blueberry Crêpes

Warm 8 ready-made crêpes, according to the package instructions. Place 2 folded crêpes on each serving plate and sprinkle each plate with 1¾ cups blueberries and 2 teaspoons vanilla sugar. Serve with one-quarter of an orange at the side of each plate, for squeezing over.

2 Caramelized Blueberry-Topped

Crêpes Fold 8 ready-made crêpes into quarters and arrange them in an ovenproof dish. Scatter over 1¾ cups blueberries, then drizzle with 6 tablespoons freshly squeezed orange juice. Sprinkle 1–2 tablespoons vanilla sugar, to taste, evenly over the crêpes, then place under a preheated broiler for 7–8 minutes, or until the sugar begins to caramelize. Serve hot with fat-free Greek-style yogurt.

10 Quick Kiwifruit and Ginger Cheesecake

Serves 4

3 oz gingernut cookies
⅓ cup low-fat cream cheese
⅓ cup low-fat crème fraîche
1 piece of stem ginger, about
    ½ oz, chopped
1 tablespoon stem ginger syrup
2 kiwifruit, peeled and sliced

- Seal the gingernut cookies in a large plastic bag and crush them using a rolling pin. Sprinkle the crushed cookies over the bottom of 4 glass serving dishes.

- Beat the cream cheese, crème fraîche, stem ginger, and syrup in a bowl, then spoon the mixture over the cookies. Arrange the kiwifruit on top of the cheesecake and serve.

 Lime Cheesecake with Kiwifruit and a Ginger Glaze Seal 3 oz gingernut cookies in a plastic bag and crush them using a rolling pin. Divide the crushed cookies into 4 tall glasses. Beat together ¾ cup extra-light cream cheese, ¾ cup fat-free Greek-style yogurt, the finely grated zest of 1 lime, and 3 tablespoons confectioner's sugar in a bowl, then spoon the mixture over the crushed cookies. Chill in the fridge for 12–15 minutes. Meanwhile, blend 2 peeled and sliced kiwifruit and 1 chopped piece of stem ginger, about ½ oz, in a food processor or blender until pulpy but not smooth. Spoon the fruit mixture over the cheesecakes and serve.

 Ginger-Marinated Kiwifruit Put 2 cups apple juice, 1 chopped piece, about ½ oz, of stem ginger, 2 tablespoons stem ginger syrup, and 2 star anise into a saucepan over medium-high heat and bring up to a gentle boil. Reduce the heat and simmer gently for 8–10 minutes until fragrant. Remove from the heat and set aside to cool. Arrange 4 peeled and sliced kiwifruit and 1 peeled, seeded, and sliced papaya on serving plates. Drizzle over the cooled syrup, and serve.

10 Raspberry Yogurt Gratin

Serves 4

3¼ cups raspberries

1½ cups fat-free Greek-style yogurt

1 teaspoon vanilla bean paste or extract

1 tablespoon cassis

2 tablespoons light brown sugar

- Preheat the broiler. Place the raspberries in an ovenproof gratin-style dish.
- Beat the yogurt with the vanilla bean paste or extract and cassis in a bowl, then spoon over the raspberries, leveling the surface.
- Sprinkle the brown sugar evenly over the yogurt mixture, then slide under the broiler for 5–6 minutes to melt the sugar. Cool slightly then serve.

2 Rasperries, Vanilla-Infused Yogurt, and Palmiers

Spread 3 tablespoons raspberry jam over a 12 oz sheet of ready-rolled puff pastry. Sprinkle 2 tablespoons brown sugar over the jam, then roll up the 2 shorter sides of the pastry until they meet in the middle. Cut the pastry log into 12 slices and place the pieces on a large, lightly greased, nonstick cookie sheet. Place the sheet in a preheated oven at 400°F for 12 minutes, or until golden. Remove from the oven and transfer the palmiers to a wire rack to cool. Beat together 1½ cups fat-free Greek-style yogurt, 1 teaspoon vanilla bean paste or extract, and 2 tablespoons raspberry jam in a bowl. Spoon the yogurt mixture into serving bowls, scatter over 1½ cups raspberries, and serve with the palmiers.

3 Raspberry and Cassis Ice

Place 1 lb frozen raspberries in a food processor or blender. Add 4 tablespoons cassis, 1 teaspoon vanilla bean extract, and just enough raspberry and cranberry juice, about ½ cup, to blend until smooth. Scrape the puree into a shallow, freezer-proof container and place in the freezer for 25 minutes. Serve with 4 vanilla shortbread cookies, if liked.

LOW-HEAL-DYP

3 Baked Nectarines with Vanilla and Cointreau

Serves 4

¼ cup Cointreau liqueur

1 teaspoon vanilla bean paste or extract

finely grated zest of ½ orange

2 tablespoons liquid honey

4 firm, ripe nectarines, halved and pitted

¾ cup fat-free Greek-style yogurt with honey, to serve

· Preheat the oven to 350°F. Put the Cointreau, vanilla bean paste or extract, orange zest, and honey in a bowl and stir until well combined.

· Arrange the nectarines, cut-side up, in an ovenproof dish, then drizzle over the Cointreau mixture.

· Put the nectarines in the oven for 18–20 minutes, or until tender, then remove from the oven and serve with the yogurt, drizzled with any juices from the pan.

1 Nectarine, Strawberry, and Orange Smoothie

Place 2 x 13 oz cans nectarines in juice in a large blender. Add 1½ cups frozen strawberries, ¾ cup freshly squeezed orange juice, and 1 teaspoon vanilla bean extract. Blend until smooth, adding a little more orange juice if necessary. Serve in tall glasses.

2 Nectarines with Vanilla Custard and a Nutty Oat Topping

In a large skillet over medium heat dry-roast ½ cup fresh bread crumbs with ½ cup rolled oats and 2 tablespoons finely chopped pecan nuts, stirring constantly until golden and crisp. Remove from the heat and stir in 2 tablespoons golden superfine

sugar. Beat together 1 cup fat-free Greek-style yogurt with honey, the finely grated zest of ½ orange, 1 teaspoon vanilla bean extract, and 8 oz fresh low-fat vanilla custard in a bowl. Remove the stone and slice 4 nectarines. Arrange the fruit in glass dishes in alternate layers with the custard mix and the crunchy oats.

30 Mulled Wine Dried Fruit Compote

Serves 4

1¼ cups light-bodied red wine

¾ cup freshly squeezed orange juice

13 oz mixed semidried fruit, such as raisins, prunes, apricots, dates, pears, and apples

½ cinnamon stick

pinch of ground allspice

pinch of ground mace (optional)

1–2 teaspoons orange blossom honey, to taste

1 tablespoon Cointreau or crème de cassis

To serve

4 tablespoons fat-free Greek-style yogurt

1½ tablespoons toasted flaked almonds (optional)

- Pour the wine and orange juice into a medium-sized saucepan and add dried fruits, cinnamon, allspice, mace, if using, and honey, to taste. Place the pan over medium-high heat and bring up to a gentle boil. Reduce the heat and simmer very gently for 10–12 minutes, stirring occasionally.

- Tip the compote into a large bowl, stir in the Cointreau or crème de cassis, and leave to cool for 10–15 minutes.

- Serve warm with a dollop of fat-free Greek-style yogurt and a scattering of toasted flaked almonds, if liked.

---

10 Mulled Wine Smoothie

In a saucepan over medium-high heat put ¾ cup red wine, ¾ cup orange juice, ½ teaspoon mixed spice, and 2 tablespoons honey. Bring to a gentle boil. Reduce the heat and simmer gently for 2–3 minutes. Put a 13 oz bag of mixed frozen fruits and 1 banana into a blender, then pour over the hot liquid and blend until smooth. Add extra honey, to taste, and pour into glasses. Serve immediately.

20 Mulled Wine Fresh Fruit Compote

Pour into a saucepan 1¼ cups light-bodied red wine and ¾ cup freshly squeezed orange juice. Place over medium-high heat and add ½ cinnamon stick, a pinch of ground allspice, a pinch of ground mace (optional), 1–2 teaspoons orange blossom honey, to taste, and 1 tablespoon Cointreau or crème de cassis. Bring up to a boil then reduce the heat and simmer gently for 10–12 minutes until fragrant.

Meanwhile, quarter 4 figs, pit and quarter 8 ripe apricots, and pit and thickly slice 2 nectarines. Add the prepared fruit with ¾ cup blueberries to the spiced wine liquid. Bring back to a simmer and cook for 4–5 minutes until the fruits soften. Cool for 8–10 minutes, then serve with a dollop of fat-free Greek-style yogurt and a scattering of toasted flaked almonds, if liked.

Index

Page references in *italics* indicate photographs

Acknowledgments

Recipes by Jo McAuley
Executive Editor Eleanor Maxfield
Senior Editor Sybella Stephens
Copy Editor Camilla Davis
Art Direction Juliette Norsworthy
Design www.gradedesign.com
Photographer Lis Parsons
Home Economist Joy Skipper
Prop Stylist Isabel De Cordova
Production Caroline Alberti